INSIDE POWER

INSIDE
POWER

GARY SHEFFIELD
AND DAVID RITZ

CROWN PUBLISHERS

NEW YORK

Library of Congress Cataloging-in-Publication Data

Sheffield, Gary
Inside power / Gary Sheffield and David Ritz.—1st ed.
1. Sheffield, Gary.   2. Baseball players—United States—Biography.
I. Ritz, David.   II. Title.
GV865.S45A3 2007
796.357092—dc22
[B]   2006101949

ISBN 978-0-307-35222-4

Printed in the United States of America

Design by Lenny Henderson

10 9 8 7 6 5 4 3 2 1

First Edition

To my grandfather, Dan Gooden, for always inspiring and motivating me, and for instilling in me a never-quit attitude and an appreciation of what it takes to be a man. I love you. Rest in peace.

Career Statistics

SEASON	TEAM	G	AB	R	H	2B	3B	HR
1988	Mil	24	80	12	19	1	0	4
1989	Mil	95	368	34	91	18	0	5
1990	Mil	125	487	67	143	30	1	10
1991	Mil	50	175	25	34	12	2	2
1992	SD	146	557	87	184	34	3	33
1993	SD	68	258	34	76	12	2	10
1993	Fla	72	236	33	69	8	3	10
1994	Fla	87	322	61	89	16	1	27
1995	Fla	63	213	46	69	8	0	16
1996	Fla	161	519	118	163	33	1	42
1997	Fla	135	444	86	111	22	1	21
1998	LA	90	301	52	95	16	1	16
1998	Fla	40	136	21	37	11	1	6
1999	LA	152	549	103	165	20	0	34
2000	LA	141	501	105	163	24	3	43
2001	LA	143	515	98	160	28	2	36
2002	Atl	135	492	82	151	26	0	25
2003	Atl	155	576	126	190	37	2	39
2004	NYY	154	573	117	166	30	1	36
2005	NYY	154	584	104	170	27	0	34
2006	NYY	39	151	22	45	5	0	6
Total	—	2229	8037	1433	2390	418	24	455

RBI	BB	SO	SB	CS	AVG	OBP	SLG	OPS
12	7	7	3	1	.238	.295	.400	.695
32	27	33	10	6	.247	.303	.337	.640
67	44	41	25	10	.294	.350	.421	.771
22	19	15	5	5	.194	.277	.320	.597
100	48	40	5	6	.330	.385	.580	.965
36	18	30	5	1	.295	.344	.473	.817
37	29	34	12	4	.292	.378	.479	.857
78	51	50	12	6	.276	.380	.584	.964
46	55	45	19	4	.324	.467	.587	1.054
120	142	66	16	9	.314	.465	.624	1.089
71	121	79	11	7	.250	.424	.446	.870
57	69	30	18	5	.316	.444	.535	.979
28	26	16	4	2	.272	.392	.500	.892
101	101	64	11	5	.301	.407	.523	.930
109	101	71	4	6	.325	.438	.643	1.081
100	94	67	10	4	.311	.417	.583	1.000
84	72	53	12	2	.307	.404	.512	.916
132	86	55	18	4	.330	.419	.604	1.023
121	92	83	5	6	.290	.393	.534	.927
123	78	76	10	2	.291	.379	.512	.891
25	13	16	5	1	.298	.355	.450	.805
1501	1293	971	220	96	.297	.398	.525	.923

Career Highlights

- Nine-time All-Star (1992–93, 1996, 1998–2000, 2003–05)
- Five-time recipient of Silver Slugger Award (1992, 1996, 2003–05)
- Ranks sixth among all active players in walks (1,293), eighth in runs (1,433), hits (2,390), and RBIs (1,501), and ninth in home runs (455)
- Number 31 in top home-run hitters of all time, behind Alex Rodriguez and Jose Canseco
- Top ten in MVP voting six times (1992, 1996, 2000, 2003–05)
- Recipient of the 2004 Thurman Munson Award for excellence on the field and philanthropic efforts off the field
- Founded the Gary Sheffield Foundation in 1997, which provides children with an environment for personal, professional, and spiritual growth
- In 1992, made a run at becoming the first National League Triple Crown winner since Joe Medwick in 1937. Sheffield led the league with a .330 average and hit thirty-three home runs with 100 RBI and a .385 on base percentage. Was honored by *The Sporting News* with the Player of the Year and Comeback Player of the Year awards
- In 2000, became the first Dodger to hit .300 with thirty homers, 100 RBI, 100 runs, and 100 walks in consecutive seasons

- Los Angeles Dodgers career leader in on-base percentage (.424), slugging percentage (.573), OPS (.998), and at-bats per home run (14.5)
- In 2003, with the Braves, smashed thirty-nine home runs and drove in 132 runs, breaking the Atlanta record of 127 set by Hank Aaron
- Shares record for home runs in an inning (two on July 13, 1997, in the fourth inning)
- Earned All-State honors in baseball during his senior year and was selected the top high school player in the nation by Gatorade
- Hit .500, averaged one home run every four at-bats, and did not strike out once in sixty-two at-bats during his senior season in high school; also posted a 6–3 record with a 1.31 ERA as a pitcher

Acknowledgments

To my mother, Betty, for encouraging me to speak the truth and always being there for me; my dad, Harold, for being a great father and accepting me as your very own; Dwight, for giving me the fire to play this game and always believing in me; and DeLeon, my wife and soul mate. I know God put us together! I don't know what I'd do without you. I love you.

Also, to my children, Ebony, Carrissa, Gary Jr., Garrett, Jaden, and Noah. You are the reason for my drive. Thank you for sharing me with the world. Everything I do is for you. And to my other mom and dad, Pastors Robert and Deborah Richards: thanks for always praying for me and receiving me as your son. To Marvet Britto (my big sis!): thanks for exposing me to life, and all the experiences along the way, as well as giving me the courage to write my story.

To Rufus Williams: Where do I begin? Thank you for your wise counsel and everything else you do (that's a book in itself!) and, most important, your support and friendship. Also, to my spiritual leaders, Bishop Randy and Paula White: thanks for never compromising. You've been instrumental in my Christian walk, not being afraid to tell me when I'm wrong and encouraging me when I'm doing right. To Bishop Noel Jones (Gardena, CA) and Bishop Eddie Long (Atlanta, GA): the two of you have been very influential in my life.

To Don Baylor: thanks for jump-starting my career and being that much-needed father figure in baseball. Also, thanks to the indispensable Donna Webster, and the team at Vigliano Associates, including David Vigliano, Kirby Kim, Mike Harriot, and Ryan Fischer-Harbage. Thanks as well to the folks at Crown Publishing, including Steve Ross, Rick Horgan, Julian Pavia, and Penny Simon.

David Ritz adds his thanks to Pops, Roberta, Alison, Jessica, Henry, Jim, Charlotte Pearl, Alden, James, Elizabeth, Sarah, Jeremy, Sam, Julia, Gabriel (the Ritz family's only baseball star), and pals Alan Eisenstock, Leo Sacks, and Harry Weinger.

INSIDE POWER

You can be shunned and scorned," my grandfather said. "You can be abused and confused, but if you have Inside Power, you have everything. Inside Power is what gets you through."

I thought Grandpa was talking about blasting the ball when they pitch it close to your body.

Turns out that was only part of it.

This business of Inside Power is the lesson of a lifetime. Fact is, it's the story of my life: how I learned it, lost it, and finally found it again; how Inside Power changed everything about me.

Don't worry, I'm not going to preach or give some lecture.

I'm just going to tell you a story about how a boy became a man.

It starts in the backyard when I'm four.

1

BUG

The summer heat was brutal. Must have been a hundred degrees, but I didn't care. I was with my uncle. My uncle was my sunshine. My uncle was letting me into his world and, man, my heart was singing.

Two little boys running around the backyards and sandlots of Tampa, Florida, 1972.

Dwight Gooden, age eight.

Gary Sheffield, age four.

Dwight was my uncle, Mama's younger brother, fourteen years younger than Mama—and to me, an only child, a big brother.

I always wanted to be in Dwight's world. He was strong and athletic. He was tall for his age and the apple of his parents'—my grandparents'—eye.

Little boys look up to big boys. Little boys want to *be* big boys.

Little boys dream big dreams, and I was no different. I wanted to run with the older guys. Wanted to do whatever they did. Wanted to get out there and show 'em I was big enough to play.

Dwight was finally letting me in. I'd been begging, he'd been resisting, and now he finally agreed.

We were going to play ball.

I'd been watching him as long as I was alive. I'd been waiting for this moment. I had the blind courage of a kid who didn't know any better. Man, I was ready.

When you're a kid, nothing matters but playing—not the stifling heat, not your scrawny body, not your raggedy little shorts. You just want to get out there and mix it up.

The dirt lot was scruffy, the ground uneven, weeds and rocks popping up everywhere.

"You stand right here," said Dwight before walking off forty-six feet, the exact distance between the mound and home plate in Little League. "You gotta catch me," he added. "I gotta practice."

Catch him? Sure, I'll catch him! I've been dying to catch him! I've been going to his Little League games and watching him pitch.

Now I'm in on the action!

We didn't have any gloves, just a white rubber ball. I crouched down in my best imitation of a catcher. Dwight wound up and let it rip. The thing came at me with such blinding speed, I jumped out of the way. It blew right past me.

Dwight laughed. "You ain't ready," he said.

"I am too. Throw it again."

I stood there, determined to hold my ground. The second pitch came in like lightning. This time I reached out to catch it, but the ball struck with such force I felt my arm rip from my shoulder. I'd never felt such pain.

"Wanna quit?" asked Dwight.

I wanted to say yes, but instead I said, "Throw me grounders," figuring grounders would be easier.

The first grounder, though, hit a rock, flew up and smacked me hard in the face. That was it. I started crying and ran inside.

"Come on," Dwight protested. "Let's keep playing."

"Mama! Grandpa!" I cried. "I don't wanna play with Dwight. It hurts to play with Dwight!"

"It's all right," said my mother, looking to console me and cuddle me in her arms.

"It *ain't* all right," said my grandfather, Dwight's dad. "The boy needs to learn. Get back out there, Bug"—Grandpa called me Bug because of my saucer-sized eyes—"and learn to catch the ball. Dwight needs to practice. Just get past the pain."

"I don't want no pain," I protested.

"Get out there!" Grandpa insisted. "Dwight's calling you."

For years Dwight kept calling me. And for years I answered the call. During those first years, I didn't want to. Didn't want to catch his fireballs. Didn't want to get popped in the eye when a grounder hit a rock and flew in my face. Didn't want to run down the ball when Dwight blasted it a mile over my head.

"Hey, Bug," Dwight kept pushing, "you wanna quit?"

He knew I did. But he also knew that Grandpa wouldn't let me.

"You can't take it anymore, can you?" he taunted.

"Yeah, I can," I said.

"Well, take *this!*"

He let loose another pitch that flew at me like a red-hot comet. If I didn't catch it, he'd laugh; if I did catch it, my hand would burn like fire.

I tried to catch it, but the ball smashed into my middle finger, bending it back till I was crying in agony.

Ran back inside. Ran back to Mama.

But Mama gave in to Grandpa who said, "Bug, get back out there."

"But I can't move my finger," I protested.

"Soak it," said Grandpa. "It'll come round."

It did.

And eventually so did I.

I stuck it out with Dwight. I sucked it up. From the very first moment I started throwing and catching a ball, I felt pressure. I had to hang in with my uncle. But it was also always something I wanted to do. Pain was part of it, but it was fun. It was all mixed together.

Pressure, pain, and fun.

How does a little kid deal with all that?

He doesn't think about it; he just keeps playing; he just wants to get better; just wants to compete with the big boys.

Day after day, spring after spring, summer after summer, fall after fall, I learned to catch my uncle's fireballs. My hands were always sore, my face bruised, but something in my spirit got strong. I wasn't going to be a crybaby.

"We ain't having no crybabies in this family, Bug," said Grandpa. "I don't wanna see you crying, and I don't wanna hear you complaining."

I learned to keep the crying on the inside; on the outside, I acted brave.

"Don't let Dwight break you," urged my grandfather. "Don't let anyone break you. Remember—you got that Inside Power."

Inside my heart, I was slowly learning to love baseball. I was getting the hang of it. I still couldn't catch most of my uncle's rockets, but once in a while I'd grab one and hold on to it for dear life. Nothing made this little boy happier.

. . .

Dwight was the center of our family's attention.

"Dwight's got what it takes," Grandpa would tell anyone who'd listen. "I do believe the boy's gonna be a star."

Everyone was proud of Dwight. And I was proudest of all. Proud to be his nephew. Proud to be seen in his company.

My uncle also intimidated me. Dwight was bigger, stronger, better at everything.

In the eyes of a six-year-old, a ten-year-old is a giant. At ten, Dwight was already famous in Little League. In my family, he was the Golden Boy.

I loved my family with all my heart. My family was everything warm and wonderful in this world.

My mom, Betty Jean, and my dad, Harold, were tight. Mom's whole life was family—her sister, her kid brother Dwight, and her parents; she was devoted to them and to me, heart and soul. Dad was a shipyard supervisor, a contractor and a construction expert. He was also a bodybuilder. No one messed with my daddy. He was my superhero.

"Your daddy ain't even your daddy," said Dwight, angry that I wouldn't go back outside to play catch. My hands were still hurting from catching him a few hours ago. I'd had enough punishment for one day.

"What do you mean my dad ain't my dad?" I asked.

"He ain't your real dad."

I was confused. I didn't even know what "real dad" meant.

"This other guy's your real dad," said Dwight. "He's a real thug. Ask your mom. You don't even know who your real dad is."

When I asked Mom, she looked at me like I'd hurt her. Then

she started tearing up. She took me in her arms and said, "I love you, and Harold loves you too, Bug, but there's another man who's your father. He's the man who I got pregnant by. If you want to meet him, he wants to meets you."

I was curious, but still unsure of what was happening. The expression "pregnant by" didn't mean a lot to me. Dwight filled in the details in a way that blew my mind. He spelled out the facts of life.

Then one day my real father showed up. He said his name was Marvin, but he never told me his last name. I just presumed it was Sheffield. He never said to call him "Daddy," and I never did.

He gave me a small stack of money. Someone said he owned a poolroom.

"Tell him you want the bills that have a hundred written on them," said Dwight, "not just ten."

I didn't want to tell the man anything. Something about him made me uneasy.

"He's toting those guns," I heard my dad Harold say. "I don't want him around Bug."

Little kids are fascinated by guns, and I was no different, but I also knew to stay away from Marvin. He'd pat me on the head, give me cash, but I never felt connected to him, not the way, say, I felt connected to my grandfather.

My grandfather was in charge of a family. The man who came by with piles of cash was in charge of a poolroom. Even a little kid called Bug knew the difference.

THE HAMMER

I was born November 18, 1968.

I was only two years old during the baseball season of 1971, when my grandfather started making me watch the Atlanta Braves on television. That year Hank Aaron hit forty-seven home runs.

"Hank is the man," said Grandpa.

Dwight, myself, and my cousin Derek were lined up on the couch. Grandpa was in his armchair, leaning forward, studying the game. He was our teacher.

"Hank is the master," Grandpa repeated over and again. "Watch his every move."

Grandpa's name was Dan Edward Gooden. He came from a little town in Georgia called Leslie. He was a big man, over six feet, 250 pounds. Grandpa had played in the semi-pros. Then a hip injury ended his career and left him with a limp. He made a living working at a chemical plant in Tampa, but his passion was baseball. He coached a few amateur teams. Mostly, though, he coached me, Derek, and Dwight. We were going to do everything he hadn't been able to do. Where he'd fallen short, we had to exceed all expectations. We'd complete what he couldn't finish. We'd carry the torch.

The pressure he felt, the pain he endured, the fun he experienced would be our pressure, our pain, our fun.

"Hank Aaron is the measure of a man," he said. "Look what he's been through. Look what he's overcome. You boys know the name of his team when he played in the Negro League?"

"No, sir."

"The Indianapolis Clowns. Now ain't that something. They take a bunch of grown men—men who had to be better than ninety percent of the white boys playing in the big leagues—and they call them *clowns*. They demean them. They disrespect them. They treat 'em like fools. They mistreat 'em like they're servants or slaves. They segregate 'em into a league so they won't make the white boys look bad. And how does Hank react to all that? My man reacts the same way Jackie Robinson reacted when they brought him up to the Dodgers in forty-seven. The Hammer reacts with his bat.

"Robinson was the same. By forty-nine, Jackie was leading the league and hitting three forty-two. Hell, by the time he hung it up, he'd played in six World Series and stolen home seventeen times. Sure, he got spat on. They called him 'nigger' practically every day of his life. They booed him and threw bottles at him. Same thing with Hank. They started booing Hank when they saw he was building up to Ruth's home run record. They don't want a black man crowned home run king. So what does the Hammer do? Goes out and hits another one. And then another.

"So study your history, boys, and learn about the men who busted down the doors for you to walk through. Larry Doby, Roy Campanella, Dan Bankhead. History's forgotten Bankhead, but Bankhead was the first black pitcher to throw in the majors. He was with Robinson on the Dodgers. Same day he makes his debut as a relief pitcher, he steps up to bat and hits it out of the park. He wasn't going to mess up his moment in the sun. No, sir, these were performers. These were pioneers. These were giants."

Grandpa would teach us history, but he would also teach us here-and-now baseball. The "Game of the Week" was our weekly lesson.

"Watch the runner on first, he's about to take off on a hit-and-run," he'd predict. Dwight and I saw how his predictions never failed.

"The outfield is too shallow," he'd say or, "The infield is too deep."

My grandfather loved strategy. He was a thinker. In technical terms, he saw the game like a chess match. "Sure, you use your body," he liked to say, "but you use your brain even more. You anticipate. If you read the pitcher right when you're hitting, you'll hit the thing. If you read the hitter right when you're fielding, you'll catch the thing. Thinking is as much a part of the game as playing. I want you boys to be *thinking* players, *smart* players. We didn't raise no fools in this family."

More and more, Grandpa included me in his baseball discussions. I loved that. Earlier, when I was four or five, all his remarks were directed at Dwight. Then, beginning when I turned six, he started speaking to both of us. Watching me play outside with Dwight, he saw that I was no quitter. I'm not saying that I didn't have many days—in fact, many weeks and months—when I would have skipped playing with Dwight if I'd had a choice. No kid likes humiliation. But the more I did it, the more I stuck with it.

Grandpa saw something else about me.

I liked to fight.

Another blistering afternoon in Tampa.

Dwight's been bugging me like crazy to go and play. I don't wanna. I wanna stay inside and watch Jackson 5 cartoons on TV.

"I won't throw hard at you," Dwight promises.

"You always throw hard," I say.

"I'll take it easy."

"No, you won't."

"Come on, Bug, I feel like throwing the ball."

"Then go ahead and throw it."

"I need you to catch me. No one else knows how."

Dwight knows how to flatter me. And the truth is, little by little, I actually am learning to catch his firebombs and sweeping curves.

We find an empty lot not far from the house. Dwight starts throwing heat. Then another kid shows up and watches. He's big—I bet he's fifteen. At the time, Dwight's twelve and I'm eight.

"Think that's a fastball?" asks the kid.

"You try and hit it," I challenge him.

The kid goes away and comes back with a bat. He's nearly six feet tall and towers over Dwight.

Dwight rears back and comes over the top.

The kid swings late and comes up with air. He calls Dwight a name. "Hey," I say, "that's my uncle."

"Shut up," says the kid, readying himself for the next pitch.

Dwight brings even more heat. This time the kid falls down swinging.

I laugh.

"I said shut up, squirt!" says the kid, who's really frustrated now.

Dwight winks at me. Dwight likes to toy with guys like this. Next pitch comes high and inside and grazes the kid on the cheek. The kid goes nuts and takes after Dwight with his bat. Without thinking, I tackle the kid from behind—all fifty pounds of me—and he falls on his face. Before he knows what's happening, I'm pounding him in the back of his head with my fist.

"Stop it, Bug," says Dwight. "You gonna hurt the guy."

"He was going to kill you," I say.

"He ain't killing no one now," says Dwight, looking down at the kid's bloody face. When he fell, he cracked his nose on a rock and split his lip. He's a mess.

I want Dwight to jump on him and hurt him more. Dwight's not thinking that way.

"If I hit him," he says, "I might hurt my arm. Gotta protect my arm."

That night we tell Grandpa the story. When he hears about me tackling the kid from behind, I can tell he's pleased. But all he says is, "Dwight did the right thing. Fighting's dangerous. He's gotta protect his arm."

Some boys are born with a fighting spirit; others aren't.

Why?

Don't know.

Where does a fighting spirit come from?

Don't know that either.

But I do know that, starting as a little kid, I approached baseball with a fighting spirit. That was just my way.

Was I angry with my uncle for keeping me sore and making me play when I was tired, hurt, and sometimes scared?

Sure I was.

Is that what gave me a fighting spirit?

I can't say. My dad Harold was a tough guy who wasn't afraid of anyone. People were afraid of him. My grandfather was also an old-fashioned macho man. He was angry that major league baseball had taken so long to let in African Americans. Did some of his anger get in me? If so, I'm glad. Far as I'm concerned, anger against injustice is good anger.

"Hank Aaron was angry," said Grandpa. "The Hammer had to be angry. But he turned the anger positive. He took it out on pitchers. When people said he could never do what the white heroes like Gehrig or Ruth did, he made them eat their words. Anger made him better."

THE CHASE

A year or so later, the chase began. Hank Aaron was closing in on Babe Ruth's home run record of 714, a number no one thought could ever be bested.

In 1973, seven of Hank's first nine hits were homers.

Grandpa got excited. "If he doesn't do it this year," he said, "next season for sure. But mark my words, this isn't going to make a lot of white fans happy."

Grandpa was right, and he was quick to read me the articles in the paper about the hate mail Hank had received.

I was a five-year-old kid and didn't understand.

"Why would anyone hate Hank Aaron?" I asked. "He's a champ."

"He's a *black* champ who's proud to be black. He ain't

scraping and he ain't bowing. There are people who can't accept that attitude."

"Why?" I wanted to know.

"Ignorance, that's why. Plain old stupidity. Most white people are fine, but there's a large and loud number of white folk who hate to see the home run record of one of their own go by the boards. They think the color of their skin entitles them to every honor. They think the color of their skin makes them superior. Well, superiority has nothing to do with skin color. It has to do with talent. And no one has more talent than Hank."

From time to time, Grandpa would read me those hate letters sent to Hank that were reprinted in the papers.

"I want you to see how much prejudice there is out there, Bug," he said. "By the time you grow up, maybe it'll be better. Or maybe it won't. But this is how it is today. They're calling him 'coon.' They're sending death threats. They're trying to get him so rattled he can't hit again. But a steady player will do what he has to do. And Hank's steady. You watch, Bug, this man has Inside Power. Inside Power is going to get him over."

In the aftermath of Aaron's hitting his seven hundredth home run, Grandpa was thrilled but also aggravated. Bowie Kuhn, Commissioner of Baseball, didn't bother to attend the game. Hank also told the press that Kuhn hadn't even sent as much as a telegram congratulating him. Hank was ticked off. So was Grandpa.

"Don't tell me that's not racism," he said. "A white player gets seven hundred homers and the Commissioner's at home plate greeting him with a dozen roses. Black man does it, Commissioner's gone fishing. Hell, last year when Hank got his three thousandth hit in Cincinnati, the Commissioner was nowhere in sight.

"But my man Hank, he's not keeping quiet about this. He's talking to the press. People are going to label him a complainer, people will tell him to stop whining, but that won't stop him. That's cause he knows he's right. He's got a genuine beef. He's being disrespected. You deliver your three thousandth hit and your seven hundredth homer and you expect a representative of the game to be there to shake your hand. That's the least they can do."

Grandpa pointed to another article that said Aaron wasn't giving his seven hundredth home run ball to the Hall of Fame.

"You know why he's not giving it to them, Bug?"

"No, sir."

"Because when he gave the Hall his five hundredth and six hundredth balls, they never acknowledged the gifts. This time Hank's saying, 'I'm tired of being disrespected. I'll keep this one for myself.' "

Grandpa kept following the chase. Every day he'd devour the sports page and watch whatever games they showed on TV.

"Look here," he said after Hank hit his 711th. "You know how many people came to see Hank play last night in Atlanta? A little over a thousand. The paper says that's the smallest crowd in Braves history. You'd think the ballpark would be sold out every night, watching this man get close to the biggest record-breaking moment in baseball history. But no. The hometown fans are staying away in droves. It's heartbreaking, Bug. It's breaking Hank's heart and it's breaking mine. This is a beautiful game, a beautiful sport, but baseball will sure enough break your heart."

At the end of the 1973 season, Aaron had tied Ruth with 714 home runs. We had to wait all winter to see him break the record in the spring.

"Waiting makes it that much sweeter," said Grandpa.

On April 8, 1974, the waiting ended. At Atlanta-Fulton County Stadium, during the Braves home opener, Hank did it. He walked in the second inning, but in the fourth, with a runner on first, he tagged Dodger pitcher Al Downing.

"It's gone!" screamed the announcer. "It's seven-fifteen! There's a new home run champion of all time! And it's Henry Aaron!"

I jumped up and down and screamed my little head off.

When I looked over at Grandpa, I saw tears in his eyes.

THE BIG LEAGUE OF
THE LITTLE LEAGUE

My folks' names are Betty and Harold Jones.

Mom asked me whether I wanted to change my name from "Sheffield" to "Jones."

"I kinda like Sheffield," I said. "It's a cool name. It's different. Is it okay if I keep it?"

"Sure," said Mom. "It's yours."

My parents and I lived way down in Port Tampa, where my father worked on the docks, before we moved to the Belmont Heights section of the city. That happened when I was eight.

Port Tampa was mostly white; Belmont Heights was black.

Port Tampa was cool. We were a happy little family. Mom and Dad got along great. All my friends were white. Living in a white world was easy for me. Didn't feel any discrimination. Liked playing with the white boys. Might have been better at football than baseball. Loved running and tackling and hitting hard. Liked jumping my bike over tires and all the other stuff the suburban boys liked to do. I fit right in.

We moved not because we were unhappy living among whites, but because of baseball. My parents and grandfather decided I needed to play in the Belmont Heights Little League. Belmont was about the best in the country and my folks wanted me to play with the best.

"The stiffer the competition," said Grandpa, "the better."

It'd be a long drive for Dad to get to work, but he was willing. Everyone was willing to sacrifice for me, and I loved them for that. I loved that Dwight wasn't the only one who the family was concentrating on, though Dwight, being the best, came first. Early on, my family saw Dwight as our ticket to a better life.

Before we got our own house in Belmont Heights, we moved in with my mom's parents for a long while, where Dwight and I shared a room. We became even closer. I was his steady sidekick.

To the outside world, we were two shy kids who stuck together like glue. Dwight was a head taller than me—lanky, agile, and fast as the wind. Everyone knew he was the baddest boy on the block. But what everyone didn't know was that I was his secret weapon.

By then I could catch him, but I couldn't hit him. No one could. It took me years before I could connect. I spent hundreds of hours swinging that stick and coming up empty. Man, I was one frustrated little guy. Eventually, though, I got used to his blinding speed and calculated my swing until I actually started to get wood on the ball.

Picture it:

Me and Dwight walking over the railroad tracks, past the industrial plant where we chase each other up and down big mounds of sand until we finally reach the street where seven big boys are waiting for us. They're all Dwight's age.

"That baby can't play," says one of the boys, pointing to me. "He'll mess up our game. Why'd you bring him?"

"I had to," says Dwight. "He's my nephew."

"He can watch," says the boy.

"If he don't play, we won't have even teams," Dwight explains.

"Then put him on *your* team," the boy insists.

"Do I have to?" asks Dwight.

"No one else wants him."

I know the game that Dwight's playing, but I still feel bad. I hate feeling like odd man out.

Stickball on the street is serious. Five on five.

For the first few innings I catch Dwight. My hand's on fire. When it comes time to hit, I can hardly hold the stick. I face a cocky pitcher a half-foot taller than Dwight. Though not as fast as Dwight, his sidearm delivery gives me fits. Fools me so bad I fall down swinging. The kids fall out laughing. I feel two inches tall. I get back up, take a deep breath and carefully time my swing. Miss by a mile. The laughs are even louder.

But next time I face the pitcher something strange happens. As I watch him wind up and go into his sidearm thing, the pitch comes at me in slow motion . . .

. . . the ball suspended in space . . .

. . . the ball rotating and rotating . . .

. . . the ball coming in close to my waist . . .

. . . the ball coming in close to my hands . . .

. . . my stick meeting the ball as it crosses the inside of the plate . . .

. . . my stick smacking the ball . . .

. . . the ball booming off the stick and flying off into space . . .

. . . the ball sailing . . . sailing . . . sailing . . .

. . . the ball sailing over the head of the pitcher, over the heads of the outfielders . . .

. . . the sight of the other boys turning their heads to follow the ball as it disappears clean out of sight . . .

Is this the Inside Power Grandpa talks so much about?

All I know is that Dwight's grinning from ear to ear.

"That's my little nephew," he proudly tells the big boys. "He's *bad*!"

Another day in the life of Bug and Uncle Dwight:

"Go into the candy store," says Dwight, "and steal me some candy."

"Do I have to?" I asked.

"You have to."

I'm Dwight's errand boy. That's great, cause it means I get to be around him all the time. And that's also rough, cause it means I gotta do his dirty work.

Anyway, I go into the store and, when the guy behind the counter isn't looking, I reach in and steal a fistful of suckers.

"Good work," says Dwight. "Now we gotta meet my mama after work."

My grandmother runs a bar on Twenty-ninth Street, but we aren't allowed in there. We're waiting outside, killing time, when one of the Crum brothers walks by. The Crums live in the hood and sometimes take us on at baseball.

"What you doing?" asks the brother.

"Waiting on my mama," says Dwight.

"I seen her working the corner down there on Osborn Street."

"No, that's *your* mama working the corner, not mine," Dwight shoots back.

"You're right. Your mama's too ugly to work the corner," the brother taunts.

"You're disrespecting my grandmother," I say, feeling fury rise up in me.

"Hey, little man," he says, laughing in my face. "Everyone knows you ain't nothing but a pimple on your uncle's ass."

I lose it. I go for him. I go for him so fast he doesn't have to time to react. I plaster him square on the chin with a nasty right. He goes down. Before he can get up, I jump on his stomach. That takes the wind out of him. He tries to push me off, but by then I land another punch that crushes his right ear and really rings his bell.

Meanwhile, Dwight's just watching.

The brother finally catches his breath, shakes his head, cusses me and goes on his way.

"You ain't fighting when someone calls your mama a name?" I ask my uncle.

"Why should I," he says, "when you're doing it for me?"

A few minutes passes before Dwight asks, "Wanna play catch?"

"My hand's hurting from hitting that guy."

"I won't throw it hard."

"That's a lie," I say.

"Come on, you're a tough guy. Let's play."

For the next half-hour, he throws that little white ball until I'm sure I've popped a blood vessel in the palm of my hand. I'm hurting so bad tears are running down my cheeks.

"I've had enough, Dwight."

"Don't move, Bug. I'm just getting warmed up."

When most kids start playing ball, it's simple. You run outside and play. You find yourself some friends and get up a game.

In my case, it was never that simple. Back then I couldn't articulate it, but I could feel it. People were counting on me—Mom,

Dad, Grandpa, Uncle Dwight. I accepted their attitude. I embraced it. After all, their attitude was a compliment to me. They were saying, "We think you've got so much talent that we're willing to change our lives around so you can get better. We're betting on you not to let us down. We believe in you."

But their attitude also weighed on my mind.

Later in life I thought of my childhood idol, Michael Jackson. He felt that kind of pressure when he was eight. The Jacksons counted on him to win singing contests and get recording contracts. You know he loved singing, just like I loved playing ball. But when adults take it to another level, when they lean on you to become not just good but the very best . . . well, that's heavy.

An only child learns to be alone. I didn't mind that. Silence never bothered me. Neither did solitude. I was attached to Mama, attached to Daddy, attached to Grandpa and Dwight, but I kept my feelings to myself. If I was worried that I might not live up to everyone's expectations, I turned that worry into determination. And I turned determination into confidence.

"You're as good as you wanna be," said Grandpa. "Good as you need to be."

I believed that.

The switch from Port Tampa to Belmont Heights was easy. I liked my white friends in Port Tampa, but moving back into a black world felt natural and comfortable. I was going home.

We lived on the edge of a bad neighborhood. The ruthless projects—Ponce De Leon and College Hill—were just around the corner. That didn't bother me. I don't remember being scared of anybody or anything. And if I was, I held the fear inside. No one knew about the fear. Not even me.

Somewhere in the mid-seventies Grandpa said to me, "Bug, you've fooled around enough. Now it's time to get serious."

Serious meant the nationally ranked Belmont Heights Little League. Serious meant trying out when I was barely eligible. Serious also meant being the youngest kid on the team. But that was nothing new for me.

Grandpa drove me over to the Little League park. He knew the coaches. In the world of Tampa baseball, Grandpa knew everyone. They saw him as the grand old man. After all, he'd produced Dwight Gooden, who'd already torn up the Belmont Heights league. I was Grandpa's Next Big Thing.

But of course I was just a little thing dreaming of becoming a big thing. My dream was to grow up and play my entire career for the Atlanta Braves, just like Hank Aaron. At the tender age of eight, I was planning a professional career. When I mentioned this to my family, they didn't laugh or call me crazy. "That's right," they said. "That's just what you're going to do."

I was a pint-size pitcher with Dwight's over-the-top delivery and Dwight's distinctive kick. I was also a pint-size catcher, the only kid in the Little League who could handle the flame-throwers. The big boys would try and intimidate me with fastballs. But for the previous four years I'd been worked over by the biggest intimidator of all. For all their speed, these guys were nothing next to Dwight.

I could also play infield. I'd been beat up by so many bad-hop grounders in dirt fields covered with rocks that the manicured green grass of the Little League looked like heaven. Scooping up ground balls was a snap.

By the time I put on my first uniform, I was prepared to do battle. I'd been through Dan Gooden/Dwight Gooden boot camp. Officially, I was nothing more than a first-year Little Leaguer. But unofficially, I was ready to move in for the kill.

HERO WORSHIP

Grandpa's limp says a lot.

You watch him walk and you see a determined man. A strong man. But a man who's been held back. His limp doesn't stop him. He goes where he needs to go. Does what he needs to do. The limp sets him apart. There's no one like my grandpa.

When he wakes me early one morning in March and says he's taking me to Al Lopez Field, home of the Cincinnati Reds' spring training, I'm the happiest kid in America. There's nothing I want to do more than watch the big leaguers practice.

Grandpa never goes out looking raggedy. He's always clean. Always immaculate. Today he's wearing a pin-striped sports coat, cool stingy-brim hat and shined-up alligators. Today he's telling me about the Reds' prospects for the 1976 season.

"They won the World Series last year," he says, "and they're going to win it again. Haven't been back-to-back world champs in the National League since the Giants did it in 1922, but count on it, Bug, the Reds are going to do it. I love me some Atlanta Braves, but let's not fool ourselves. No one can compete with the Reds' Big Eight. Can you name the Big Eight, Bug?"

"Yes, sir," I say.

"Go on, son."

I take a deep breath and name the names: "Johnny Bench, Pete Rose, Joe Morgan, Tony Perez, Dave Concepcion, George Foster, Ken Griffey, Cesar Geronimo."

"Perfect. Now let's go see them play."

Walking into the ballpark, my heart's thumping like crazy. Al Lopez Field lets you get super close to the players. I sit in the first row on the first base side, my eyes glued on Pete Rose at second.

First batter up lines a scorcher to Rose's right. Pete grabs it and throws him out. Me and Grandpa cheer. Second batter check-swings a little dribbler to the right of the pitcher's mound. Rose has to rush in to scoop it up and flip to first. Out! Charlie Hustle does it again. Third man hits an easy ground ball right at Rose. No problem. I'm thinking that Pete's going to put out all three hitters in this first inning. But just as I'm thinking that, the ball goes through Pete's leg. Amazingly, Pete has committed an error.

I'm stunned. I don't think major leaguers ever make mistakes. But as soon as the error is made, my grandfather, along with everyone else in the park, is up on his feet, yelling, "That's okay, Pete, you'll get it next time . . . no problem, just a bad hop . . . hang in there, Pete, no big deal."

The memory of the fans at Al Lopez Field cheering on Pete Rose after that error would stay with me for the rest of my life. As a young boy, I learned that the job of the baseball fan is to cheer their heroes, even during bad times. As a young boy, I was taught that players, especially those skilled enough to be in the majors, are to be revered, honored and encouraged, especially when the going gets rough.

When you're raised around strong men, your focus is on being strong yourself. In the eyes, mind, and soul of a little boy, strength makes a man.

Little boys first understand physical strength. Physical strength means power. Watching my dad lift killer weights motivated me to do the same. Of course, I couldn't. I couldn't maneuver the dumbbells and barbells, but when he wasn't looking I tried. I'd look in the mirror and strike a pose. I'd fantasize about benching five hundred pounds. I'd pretend I was Superman.

Every morning Dad ran ten miles before work. Then at night he'd work on the house, the plumbing, the yard, the electricity. You name it, Dad did it. When we finally moved from my grandfather's into a place of our own—that happened when I got to high school—it was a house built by Dad's own hands. Dad was all about work and caring for his family. Everyone who knew him liked him, respected him, called him a real man.

Protecting Mama and me was his first priority, but my daddy had his own notion of protection.

I found that out when I came home early one evening with a black eye and bloody nose. Happened when I was nine or ten.

"What happened?" Dad wanted to know.

"Got in a fight with a guy, but then three of his friends jumped me," I said.

"All at once?"

"Yeah," I said, "all at once."

Dad didn't say anything. He just went and got his gun.

"Get in the car, Bug," he ordered.

I got in the car, not knowing what to expect.

"Tell me where it happened," said Dad.

I pointed out the empty lot. The boys were still there, all four of them.

Dad got out of the car, drew his gun and pointed at them.

"If you knuckleheads wanna fight my boy," he said, "you gonna fight him fair. One at a time. So get started."

One by one, I faced each of them down. I was quicker with my fists than any of them. By the time I faced the fourth guy, though, I was tired enough to pass out. But something kept me going. I was dead set on showing Dad what I was made of. With my last burst of strength, I threw the kid to the ground and kicked him in the stomach. He groaned loudly and started to cry.

"Let's go," said Dad. "You made your point."

At dinner Mama asked Daddy, "What happened to Bug today?"

"Bug got tougher today," said Dad. "A lot tougher."

DREAMS

I'm dreaming of having a little brother who'll look up to me. I'm dreaming of having friends my own age who won't torment me.

I'm dreaming of playing football where I don't have to take orders from Dwight, where I don't have to play linebacker and take the hits.

I'm dreaming of growing up and having a girlfriend who'll become my wife. I'm dreaming of having kids and living happily ever after.

I'm dreaming of playing major league ball and becoming the next Hank Aaron.

I'm dreaming of making Mom, Dad, Grandpa, and Grandma proud of me.

I'm dreaming of beating up the bully who's terrorizing the neighborhood.

The last dream came true first.

I forget the name of the bully. But I sure remember how he went around bragging. He said he could whip anyone. He picked on kids smaller than him. But even though I was smaller, I was building muscle. My legs were getting strong and, in my spirit, I was ready to take on anyone.

"Not this guy," said Dwight. "Leave this guy alone."

Dwight was always nonconfrontational. Me, I couldn't wait for the confrontation. I was ready when the bully came at me in the schoolyard. First he came at me with words: threatening words, dirty words. I told him to back off.

"Make me," he said.

I went for his gut. I landed a little high, but I hit him so hard I cracked one of his ribs. Before he knew what hit him, he was down. He was stronger than me, but I was quicker. And when he was down, I made a mess of his face. They had to pull me off.

After that, my reputation was made.

Today when you hear the word "gang," you think guns, drugs, and murder.

Back in my day, gangs were just groups of kids protecting a territory. We didn't even have knives. We used our fists. We called ourselves the Alley Cats because our sacred ground was this one little alley. Other gangs entered at their own risk.

My real sense of belonging, though, wasn't tied to the Alley Cats. It was tied to the Belmont Heights Little League. I knew the Alley Cats weren't going to make my dreams come true. But the Little League just might. The Little League was where I could put my aggression to good use. It's where Grandpa and Dad came to see me perform. It's where, in my own little way, I first became a star.

I'm not sure it's good for a kid to be a star. Your ego gets jacked up; your pride swells; your innocent heart is no longer innocent. You crave glory.

But as a kid, I wasn't analyzing. I was just going for it. It was all set out there before me. If my uncle could do it, so could I.

As I got into double digits—age ten—I started getting good. I made the Little League team. Of course I wasn't paid, but it sure felt like the start of my professional career. I was no longer just playing for fun. I was playing for keeps. This was serious stuff.

So serious, in fact, that our team got famous. In 1980, we slugged our way into the Little League World Series. I was all of eleven, and I was going to be on national television. ABC's *Wide World of Sports* was covering the game live.

We couldn't lose. We were just too strong for any team to contend with. We'd muscled our way through an amazing season where I excelled, sometimes pitching, sometimes catching, but always hitting up a storm. I'd found my groove as a player and was determined to dominate every game. My teammates included Derek Bell, future big leaguer. Derek was a better player than me. So was Tyrone Griffin, who years later wound up a first-round draft pick of the Chicago Cubs.

We got to Williamsport, Pennsylvania, where we were scheduled to face Taiwan. We weren't worried. It was just a matter of how bad we'd beat them.

When we first saw the Taiwanese players, we were a little taken aback. They didn't look like boys. They looked like men.

They were big and burly and no one could tell me that they weren't fourteen or fifteen, way past the Little League cutoff.

"Don't matter," I told my teammates. "We're destroying them."

Day before the game, we went to the recreation room to play Ping-Pong. There were three tables, and the Taiwanese team was using all three. Cool. We'd wait. But after a half hour, they didn't relinquish even one table. We said we wanted to play. They acted like they didn't understand, but we understood they did.

"Give us a table," we said, "or we'll kick your butts."

They didn't budge.

I shoved one of the big guys. He shoved me back. One of his teammates started mouthing off. I couldn't understand him, but I knew whatever he was saying wasn't pretty. One of our guys got kicked. That was it; all hell was about to break loose when a league official stepped between us.

"See you jerks on the field tomorrow," we said. "We're gonna put a hurting on you that you won't forget."

Tomorrow came and we were ready. Fourteen tough kids from black Tampa weren't about to be intimidated by anyone.

I was behind the plate, my pal Kirk Walker on the mound. We taunted the hitters. We had trash-talking raps designed to rattle. We had it down.

Underneath the attitude, though, we also had a bad case of the nerves. That showed up when, in the first inning, we made three errors that led to two runs. For all our brashness, we never recovered.

Tyrone Griffin smacked a homer in the first. But Taiwan came back in the third with two round-trippers. I hit a line-drive double in the third and eventually scored on a slick hook slide home, but it wasn't enough. We lost 4–3.

We cried.

All of us—tough and rough boys from the hood—cried our little eyes out. It was my first taste of national humiliation.

We felt that we'd let the whole city down, including our families and friends. In Tampa, we were the pride of the community. When we won, merchants would buy us new uniforms and pay for improvements on our playing field. When we lost, no one was inclined to give us anything.

Dejection is part of playing ball. You lose and you get the blues. But when you're a kid and lose in a very public way—like on national TV—you don't have the emotional resources of an adult. You can't rationalize. You can't shake it off. You can't stop crying.

All you can do is start thinking: *Next year, next year, next year.*

Next year we'll win.

Next year we'll be back.

And we were.

Except I wasn't there.

THE INCIDENT

Twenty-five years after it happened, the incident still haunts me. I finally gave up the rage and resentment, but, man, I kept it bottled up for a long time. It lit a fire inside me that kept burning, burning, burning.

I was twelve.

After our loss to Taiwan, the Belmont Heights Little League team was determined to come back and win it all. We were going to practice harder, play harder, stay focused. No one could stop us.

Season went great. I was catching and pitching; I was flowing with confidence. And while our team was tearing up the Little League, Uncle Dwight was tearing up the Senior League. At sixteen, he was famous all over the state. His ERA was .75. No one could touch him. This was around the time when a fan, watching

Dwight come over the top with a scorching fastball, yelled, "Strike him out . . . operate on him, Doc."

From then on, Dwight was Doc.

Doc was pitching a big game on a Saturday afternoon. Always proud of my uncle, I wanted to watch him operate. Only problem was that I had Little League practice.

I figured my coach might be miffed, but he'd understand.

So I went and watched my uncle mow down the opposition. He pitched a shutout masterpiece that had me glowing with pride.

After the game I went home.

"Your coach was looking for you," said Mom. "He said you missed practice. Where were you?"

"At a friend's house," I said. "He was helping me with homework."

Mom bought the lie.

The following Monday I was scheduled to pitch our next Little League game against our biggest rival. The game was important because if they beat us we'd fall into a tie for first place. I had my heart set on doing just what Doc had done: I was going to throw a shutout.

"Gary," said the coach, when I arrived in time for batting practice. "Where were you Saturday?"

"Sorry, coach, I had too much schoolwork."

"You missed practice. You missed it without permission. You can't do that, son. If you were sick, I'd understand. If it was a family emergency, I'd understand."

"But it was schoolwork, coach—"

"Understood. But that doesn't change anything, Gary. You broke our rule and I'm going to have to discipline you. You can't pitch today. I'm benching you."

"You can't."

"What was that?"

"You can't."

"Look, little man," he said, "I'm the coach. I can do what-ever I want to do."

Something snapped in me. I saw red. Red like blood. I started screaming. *"I gotta pitch! You said I was the only one who could beat this team! You said it yourself! You gotta let me pitch!"*

"A decision's a decision, son, and this one has been made. Just sit down."

At that moment I lost it. Instead of sitting down, I found myself running to the bat stand, grabbing a metal bat, and wav-ing it over my head like I was going to hit the coach.

I never got the chance. My teammates restrained me, held back my arms and took the bat out of my hands.

The coach saw all this, his eyes widening in fury. He came over, got in my face and practically spit these words out at me.

"You'll never play for this team again! Ever!"

"You can't do that," I said.

"Watch me."

And with that, he stormed off.

I didn't believe him. The team counted on me too much to let me go. I could pitch, catch, field, and hit. The team wanted so badly to get back to Williamsport and win the World Series that they wouldn't think of trying to make it without me.

I couldn't be kicked off the team.

Impossible.

Bad dream.

Not really happening.

Ran home and told Dad. Meanwhile, Dad had tracked down my lie about schoolwork. He confronted me. I confessed. He said I was grounded for two weeks.

"Okay," I said. "I can deal with that. But I gotta play."

"What did you do that upset the coach?" asked Dad.

In rough terms, I told him.

"You *what!*" said my father. "You picked up the bat!"

"Picked it up," I said, "but didn't do anything with it. Never touched him."

"Gary," said my father, "you operate on a short fuse."

Ran to my grandfather. Told him what had happened. He said I was wrong, but he'd speak to the coach.

He did, but the coach wasn't changing his mind. I was off the team for the entire year.

For what? For losing my temper for a hot second? Wasn't right, wasn't fair. I had to turn it around.

Talked to my teammates, but what could they do? Sure, they wanted me on the field, but the coach was the coach.

Talked to some of the other coaches.

"Sorry, Gary," they said. "You dug your own grave."

I felt like I was dying. Or already dead. No baseball, no life. Without a starting position on the Belmont Heights Little League team, there was no point in living.

Sitting out the season was like living in hell.

I didn't give up: I convinced other grown-up men to beg the coach on my behalf, but they couldn't convince him.

Getting more desperate, I tried to switch into another Little League, but Belmont Heights blocked me.

So there I was, age twelve, boiling in a stew of rage, the first of many to come. At the time, of course, I thought I was right. I thought the coach had overreacted. Punish me, sure. Bench me for a game, or a week, or even a month. But whatever you do, don't keep me from the World Series. The World Series was where I was going to catch, pitch, and slug my team to glory. The World Series was where I'd make the city of Tampa—the entire state of Florida—proud of me. The World Series was where I'd shine.

Instead I sulked.

Day and night, night and day. Deep down despair.

The despair deepened, I suppose, when I saw that my team was succeeding without me. I was happy for them; I never stopped rooting for Belmont Heights—still do to this day—but I couldn't help but feel useless. They had a great season and, just like that, got to go back to Williamsport in June. They made it to the World Series. They faced that same team of rough and tough Taiwanese kids who were too big to be kids.

I had to watch the game on TV. Grandpa was by my side. He knew enough not to say anything to me. We watched in silence.

Adding insult to injury, we got beat again, 4–3. I couldn't help feeling that I could have made a difference. Sure, that may have been ego talking, but my ego, even as a preteen, talked loud and long.

But was it ego, or was it confidence?

Was it arrogance or self-assurance?

Whatever it was, it wouldn't keep quiet.

I had something to prove. The coach had kept me from doing the one thing I had to do. I had to do it because everything and everyone drove me to it—my grandpa, my dad, my mom, my uncle Doc. The world drove me to it. My own heart drove me to it. I had to play. I had to win. I had to prove that I could mix it up with the big boys.

I *had* to.

STRANGE AUCTION

I was thirteen and in the Senior League. No matter what league, Belmont Heights was the bomb. I put all my frustration from being denied that trip to Williamsport into improving my game. And I did improve. I grew a couple of inches in height. I gained muscle. I concentrated on fielding as well as pitching and hitting. I could play short and second. I could catch. Felt like I could do it all.

I accomplished a lot that year. I helped our team get to the Senior League World Series in Taylor, Michigan. I was back in the game. Missing Williamsport the year before still hurt, but the fact that I'd fought my way back into big-time kids' baseball made me feel good.

I'd said they couldn't keep me down, and they couldn't.

Come summer, the all-black Belmont Heights team flew to

Michigan. When we were driven to a hotel and put in a big ball-room, I got the shock of my life.

We were auctioned off.

I'm not kidding. We were asked to stand in the middle of the room—all fourteen or fifteen of us—facing a large group of white people, mothers and fathers with their children. These people had all heard of Belmont Heights because we were famous in Little League and Senior League baseball circles. They'd paid big money for the honor of hosting us in their homes during World Series week. Now they got to choose which of us would go off with them and their family.

It was all for a good cause—the money they'd paid for us created revenue for the Belmont Heights Senior League. But man, I gotta tell you, it felt like a slave auction: us just standing there, being looked over and then selected by a bunch of strange white folks.

You'd think someone—our people or theirs—would have had more sensitivity than to expose us to this. But hey, this is America. I was learning that in America racial sensitivity isn't exactly at the top of the menu.

Anyway, I was chosen by a family and carted off to the burbs. Nice house, nice family, but filled with oversized cats. I didn't like cats because a nasty cat had once gone after me. Fact is, I was afraid of cats. Now I was surrounded by them. So I spent most of my time in the guest room hiding out.

The family asked me what I wanted to eat. I told them that I liked pizza. But when the pizza came, they put it in the refrigerator to cool off.

"Cold pizza?" I asked.

"That's how we eat here."

"Well, in Tampa we eat it hot."

And so it went. The whole thing couldn't have been more uncomfortable.

But I took all those awkward feelings: my fear of cats, the weirdness of being pawned off like a slave, and turned it into fury on the field.

Belmont Heights played like a house on fire.

I pitched the final game, the one for the Senior League World Championship. I pitched my heart out and won hands down.

I was ready for high school.

"HIGH SCHOOL HAUNTS YOU FOREVER"

That's what a friend of mine told me.

"High school," she said, "is where you're formed. Your friends, your goals, your values—it all comes together in high school."

No doubt, high school is deep. High school is where your dreams get serious. My dreams of eventually having a beautiful wife and a beautiful family hadn't changed. Like my hero Hank Aaron, I'd play my whole career with the Atlanta Braves and live in a big home with a pool in the back. I'd buy my folks a house and make enough money so Dad could retire. Life would be simple: family and baseball, baseball and family. Life would be perfect.

High school started off great. I had a girlfriend named Davine who was pretty and sweet. We were in love, or at least that thing

43

teenagers call love. I had my fifty-zipper Michael Jackson leather jacket. I even had a gold cap on one of my teeth. Back then, that's how I rolled.

It's unusual for a freshman to make the varsity baseball team, especially at Hillsborough High. Like the Belmont Heights Little League, Hillsborough had a big-time reputation as one of the best baseball programs anywhere. Doc had enjoyed a great career at Hillsborough. In fact, just about the time I was getting in, he was getting out. Doc was being drafted by the Mets. It was an amazing moment for our family.

Doc didn't use an agent. He used his dad. This was going to be interesting. My grandfather wasn't a lawyer. He wasn't a professional negotiator. He was a guy who worked in a chemical plant. At the same time, we were convinced that no major league scout, no matter how slick, could outsmart or intimidate Dan Edward Gooden. The man was iron.

The first signing bonus offer was forty thousand dollars. Grandpa said, "You're way off. Forget it." Doc went crazy. He couldn't believe his dad was turning down that much money. The next offer was seventy thousand. Doc was ready to jump at it. Remember, we were regular working people. This kind of money was a fortune to us. But my grandfather didn't get carried away. "I know my son's value," he told me. "If they're willing to pay him seventy thousand, they'll pay him eighty-five thousand."

Which is what Doc got, all because of his father's steely confidence.

When I watched it go down, I could feel that confidence seep into me.

This is my heritage.

These are my people.

This is the grandfather who raised me.

I was proud.

. . .

I was so proud of the Gooden tradition that I was determined to go to Hillsborough High School, where Doc had made his mark. By then my folks and I lived in the King High School district. Dad had moved us to a better neighborhood, and King had a good baseball team, but it wasn't Doc Gooden's team. I couldn't even think about any other high school except Hillsborough. I went through all kinds of changes, made all sorts of petitions, and was finally told that if I joined ROTC at Hillsborough I'd be admitted. "Fine," I said. "Where do I sign up?"

Some said only squares and nerds joined ROTC, but I didn't care. I had to get into that high school and follow in my uncle's footsteps. No point in trying to tell me otherwise.

I joined ROTC. I got into Hillsborough. And best of all, I made the varsity baseball team freshman year. I did so with a little calculation. Though I knew I'd always excelled as a pitcher and catcher, there was no way I could make the team that way. The older guys had those positions locked up. Watching them practice, I saw that my best chance was second base. The infield had never been my prime territory, but baseball was baseball. Grandpa taught us that you should be able to play anywhere. Following his philosophy, I went after the second base job. I could handle the grounders. I could make the double plays. I could play second all day long. I got it.

In class, I was a questioner. I didn't trust the history books. When we studied what had happened in America, I was aware that we were reading a white man's version. When we studied World War II, for example, they didn't tell us about how the

German prisoners of war brought to the American South were treated better than the African American workers in the fields. My grandfather told me many of those stories. The story of discrimination against blacks in sports, for example, never made its way into the books.

The teachers thought I was a pain. I didn't take anything at face value. I knew there was more to the story than the white-bread version. Why weren't we given books about black heroes? Why were we being fed only one point of view?

"That's enough," said one of the teachers when I wanted to know why black men were drafted to fight in the great wars of this century while they were still being lynched back home. "You're disturbing the class," she said.

That's because something about American history was disturbing me.

The competition among Tampa high schools was fierce. It was a situation similar to the Little League and Senior League. This was baseball played by kids, but it was serious stuff. The drive to survive in this hotly contested atmosphere was intense. But it was also fun. It was what I wanted. I was living out Dan Gooden's dream: he didn't just have a son who had the potential to hit the big time. He had a grandson—two, in fact, because my cousin Derek was also doing great.

Looking back, remembering the competition I faced during those years, I'm amazed by the names: Derek Bell, Tyrone Griffin, Tino Martinez, Luis Gonzales. At ages fourteen, fifteen, and sixteen, these were the guys from rival high schools. When I played them, people would line up to see if I could do it as a pitcher *and* as a hitter.

At the same time that I was struggling to make my name as

a high school star, Doc was exploding as a major league star. In 1984, my sophomore year, Dwight set a major league rookie record with 276 strikeouts in 218 innings. He went 17–9, had an ERA of 2.60, and was named Rookie of the Year. He turned the Mets into contenders. The next year, when I was a junior, he did even better. My uncle became a national sensation. He walked away with the Cy Young Award. He also won the triple crown of pitchers by winning the most games (24) and having the lowest ERA (1.53) and the most strikeouts (268). "Doctor K" banners, recording his strikeouts, were popping up all over Shea Stadium—in fact, all over the country.

Doc never forgot me. In fact, Doc liked to boast about me. He'd say, "I have this nephew down in Tampa who's going to be something." I was still his secret weapon. The big difference, though, was that in our childhood Dwight liked to show me off in front of his friends, the older guys. But now his friends were Darryl Strawberry and Eric Davis. Now his friends were world-famous superstars. But Doc's attitude about me hadn't changed.

During a high school game in my junior year, I looked up and there was my uncle watching me approach the plate. Standing next to him were Strawberry and Davis. Stars were in my eyes. Dreams were in my head. I tried not to lose my cool. I stood up there and concentrated on the guy throwing the ball, not on Doc and his pals. The first pitch was inside, just where I like it. I smoked it. I drove it into the left field stands. My soul smiled. My heart sang. My uncle turned to his famous friends and cried out, "Told you so!"

RED CORVETTE

Senior year changed everything. I could divide my life into before and after my senior year.

Before, the dream held steady. I'd play for the Braves, the team of my dreams. I'd marry the woman of my dreams and we'd have a dream family. The American dream was coming my way.

But it missed me, or I missed it, I'm not sure which. Either way, my life didn't go the way I wanted. In many ways, it went great. You'll see that there were big changes and big excitement. You'll see that success seemed to be mine. So why didn't happiness accompany that success? What happened to turn things around? Why did the dream die out even before it got started?

It wasn't drugs or drink. The one time I drank beer my senior year I got myself sick. I drank it like it was water, mug after mug, and wound up vomiting my guts up. I hated the feeling of not being in control. It'd be a long time before I'd even look at the stuff again.

I hated drugs. When I saw my boys high, on weed or whatever, they acted like fools. Their conversations turned silly and their minds turned cloudy. They said and did things that were out of character. They made bad mistakes and I could see that something besides good judgment was in charge of their decision-making. I wanted no part of screwed-up decision-making. I wanted control.

My decision to pursue my dream was, far as I could see, foolproof. *I* was in charge. *I* was getting to go where *I* needed to go based on my own power. That power and prestige doubled the day Doc decided to give me the red Corvette he'd been driving.

The fact it was a hand-me-down only made it sweeter. It was Doc's way of saying, "You deserve this. You'll be next. These are the toys that the great players get, and you're a great player. Take this Corvette as my vote of confidence."

Man, no one has ever been more grateful. No nephew has ever loved an uncle more. Everyone at school knew where the car came from—and that made it special. Even better, when Doc came to town, he'd take me with him on his interviews. I'd sit in the corner while famous broadcasters asked him questions. He'd let me hang with him and Eric Davis.

Eric was about the most down-to-earth guy I'd ever met. Talked real. Walked real. And was the cleanest dresser in the big leagues. Eric had style, something I've always loved. Eric wore a leather shirt and matching leather shorts, the toughest outfit you could imagine.

I appreciated on-the-field style, too—for example, Barry Larkin's style at shortstop. He joined the Reds when I was a high school senior. Larkin was the complete player. He'd go on to be in twelve All-Star games with a lifetime batting average of .295.

He never played for anyone except the Reds, giving me another example of how to shape a career. One team forever. Plus, Larkin was a brilliant fielder. He owned his position and was steady, strong, and spectacular when he needed to be. I wanted to be Larkin.

While I was still in high school, Doc invited me to New York. I got to visit the Mets locker room and ride on the team bus. There was Straw, Gary Carter, Keith Hernandez, Mookie Wilson, Len Dykstra, Bob Ojeda, Sid Fernandez. I was tripping. The trip got even heavier when Doc took me to his luxury apartment and showed me his walk-in closet, where he had twenty pairs of shiny new Freeman's shoes lined up by color and style.

When it came time for the alumni game at Hillsborough, the whole school was buzzing. Doc was back, face to face with Bug. Uncle was going to make nephew look bad. Everyone and his mother turned out for the game. Doc's big point of pride that day was that he smacked a line-drive homer off me. My big point of pride was that, though he tried his hardest, he never struck me out. I didn't get a hit, but I never went down swinging. I got a piece of the ball every time.

Doc loved coming home to Tampa, home to the high school and family he cared about most. One of those trips, though, turned bad. It also happened my senior year. Twenty years later, people are still talking about that night.

Dwight invited me and a group of friends to a University of South Florida basketball game. Just before we left, Doc's mom, my grandmother, said, "Boys, why don't you stay home? I don't have a good feeling about tonight."

There'd been racial tension in Tampa between police and the black community, and Grandma saw her son as a target because of the way he rolled—he didn't mind showing off his fancy cars.

"Don't worry, Mama," Dwight assured my grandmother, "we'll be fine."

We went to the game in a caravan of four cars. The USF game was fun, but we felt the eyes of the police staring at us the whole time. We didn't know why. We weren't drinking heavily. We weren't carrying on. Of course, Doc was the center of attention. Everyone was coming by for a picture or a handshake. And so were the cops. They were all around us.

After the game we went to Bennigan's. Again, fans congregated around Doc. Again, we did nothing wrong. I was enjoying the leftover limelight of my uncle's fame. So far, so good, although it was weird how the cops were following us as if we'd robbed a bank.

"We're outta here," said Doc, sensing we'd better end the evening sooner rather than later.

We got into our cars and headed home. My Corvette led the way, Doc's car right behind me. We came to a green light that turned yellow as we entered the intersection. Seeing a cop car nearby, I decided to back up rather than run the risk of getting a ticket. We waited patiently. When the light turned green, we drove on. That's when the cop pulled me over. I had no idea what he wanted. And he didn't seem to know either. Just routine questions about nothing in particular.

Out of the corner of my eye, I saw that Doc's car had also been pulled over. A few minutes later, when I turned around to see what was happening with my uncle—I figured he was being hassled same as me—I saw the cops taking him to the ground. That's when I exploded. First thing I thought was, *They're going to break his arm!* So I ran over, knocked down four or five cops, and picked up Doc off the ground. That's when the cops went after us with a vengeance, beating us with their nightsticks. Our only weapons were our fists, and our fists weren't enough. We got beat up bad.

We spent the night in jail. You talk about rage! We were sure the reason the cops had focused on us was that they were jealous of Doc's fame and figured he flaunted it with fancy cars. A lawyer got us out. Charges were dropped. Eventually Dwight sued the police and won, but not before the city of Tampa exploded.

Word got out. The black neighborhoods were as incensed as we were. Doc was a hero and Doc had been attacked for no reason. Attack Doc and you attack every African American in Tampa. The city broke out in riots. The police wanted us to call for peace and calm things down. But we weren't feeling peaceful and we weren't calm. We were filled with anger at being beaten for no earthly reason. Eventually the neighborhoods quieted, but the bitterness lasted. Although Doc was a homeboy who loved his native city, he never felt the same about Tampa again. The wounds from this incident were ugly, painful, and deep.

HUMAN NATURE

Michael Jackson had a song about it on *Thriller,* the record everyone was listening to when I was a teenager. Human nature is something else. It'll take us to one place, then another. My human nature in high school was focused on two things—baseball and girls. Baseball came first. I knew that baseball was my gift and my way into the world. Baseball was my heritage and baseball was my blood. But so was my feeling for women.

I had several girlfriends, but Davine was my steady from seventh grade on. Davine was cool. And then senior year I met Linda.

Linda was fine. I met her through my family; her mother was my grandmother's friend. My parents thought we'd make a great couple, and so did I. Linda was a model. Beautiful personality, everything I wanted in a girl. We hooked up and became inseparable. Linda would make my dream come true.

I picked her up in my red Corvette and took her to work every day after school. The man who owned the modeling agency noticed that I was always on time. He also owned a big barbecue stand where the Tampa Bay Buccaneers hung out. He gave me a job there serving food and cutting up beef. Everything was great.

Linda and I talked about family, marriage, our life together. The stars were in place. What could go wrong?

I was a young senior, only sixteen, but felt like I had my game down. I hit the most home runs in a twenty-game season— fifteen—and went up against powerhouse pitchers and hitters. More and more, the scouts came around. Every big game you'd see them gather on East Cayuga, right next to our field, to watch me play. Afterwards they'd congregate at Nico's Diner. They were friendly to me. A few contacted my dad. There was action. The big leagues were interested. As the year went on, I grew more excited. I was hitting well and pitching well. And out of the corner of my eye I couldn't help but see the scouts continuing to line up, watching my every move.

"I want to start a family," I said to Linda. "I think the Braves are going to sign me. I think they'll give me a big bonus, and I want you to be a part of it all."

"Gary," said Linda. "I love you, baby. I want whatever you want."

I wanted it all.

So when we learned that Linda was pregnant, I rejoiced. The

plan was working out, the dream coming true. We were going to live happily after ever.

Until two things happened:

The Atlanta Braves did not sign me.

And the perfect life that I'd planned had collapsed.

It was all over before it began.

BONUS BABY

The term sounds great. What high school baseball player doesn't want to be a bonus baby? I sure did. And even though the Braves didn't want me, the Milwaukee Brewers did. Not only did they want me, they offered a $150,000 bonus.

I know I was feeling pain for not being signed by Atlanta, and I know that I hid that pain, but it was hard not to be happy when at least one big league team came up with a big check. Besides, everyone in Tampa learned that I'd been signed—it was in all the papers—and everyone was telling me I was a winner.

"Atlanta's loss is Milwaukee's gain," said my grandfather. "Besides, Hank Aaron started out in Milwaukee."

"You've proven yourself," said Dad.

"We couldn't be more proud of you, son," said Mama.

All the celebration was cool; all the articles about me jacked up my ego; all the kids in Hillsborough offering me high fives was nice. But the truth was that my personal life was a confusing mess.

The mess had begun when my mom started hearing rumors that I had a baby out there. Mama didn't pay any attention, and neither did I. Then one day she opened a letter addressed to me saying that Davine had applied for assistance for herself and the child she'd had with me. What child? After we'd broken up, Davine had never said a word about being pregnant. So I had my doubts.

Then Mom got a call from Davine's cousin, who swore it was true. She said that the baby was mine. That's when my mother— a strong, protective, and decisive woman—took matters in her own hands. She got Davine's address and said, "Gary, we're going over there."

We got to the house where Davine lived with her dad.

"Wait in the car," Mama told me.

Mama went in, took one look at the three-month-old baby girl named Ebony, and came out and got me.

"That child," she said when I walked into the house, "is yours." There was no arguing. Mom was right. The resemblance was strong.

"We're going to do the right thing," Mama told Davine and her dad. "We're honorable people and my son is an honorable man."

As it would turn out, my mother and father would raise Ebony.

Meanwhile, though, Linda couldn't be consoled until Mama sat her down. Mama did the math and proved that I'd broken up with Davine before I'd started going with Linda. Linda couldn't argue with the numbers. She saw that I hadn't cheated on her.

Unfortunately, our relationship changed. Over time, it seemed like she turned into a different person. I no longer saw Linda and

Gary as the perfect couple about to have the perfect marriage. She remained my girlfriend, but I no longer wanted to get married.

So there I was, graduating high school, going into professional baseball, and about to be the father of two babies.

Carissa, my second daughter, was born eleven months after Ebony.

And the strangest part was this:

In the middle of all this activity, all these relationships, all these changing lives, I found myself completely alone.

HELENA, MONTANA

Loneliness is a heavy thing.

Loneliness can weigh on you night and day.

Loneliness can have you crying into the night, crying for your mother, crying for your father and your grandfather, crying for home.

When I look back, I see that when I went into the pros, I was more a boy than a man. I was still tied to Mama, and would be for many years to come. I was still tied to my father and grandfather and the security of being known in Tampa as a star.

Helena, Montana, might have been on the other side of the moon for all I knew. I had to look on the map to find it. And when I got there, I felt like I *was* on the moon. Man, it was strange territory.

First off, I moved from a black world to a white one. When

my white friends asked me what was so difficult about that, I said, think about it in reverse. Imagine if you were a white boy brought up somewhere like All-White, Indiana. Your family is white, everyone in school is white, your girlfriends are white, your teachers, preachers, teammates, coaches, competitors. Your world is white. Then suddenly you're drafted by a team and plunked down in the middle of All-Black, Georgia, where there's not a white face in sight. Even all the fans are black. Wouldn't that freak you? Wouldn't that make you go through some changes?

Well, brother, I went through some changes in Helena, Montana. Wasn't an easy transition. Emotionally I was messed up because I was leaving two babies behind. Part of me was relieved because I was hardly equipped to deal with the responsibility. Going off to the Brewers farm system was a great excuse to escape. I had to make money; I had to make my career; I had to go. But another part of me felt guilty. Mama and Daddy were caring for Ebony, and Linda was caring for Carissa.

I loved my kids and, as time went on, I was there for them, not just financially but also emotionally. In the beginning, though, I was just a kid having kids. I was still learning what it meant to be a man. Later I sat down with my mom and dad and asked them: How do I teach my kids wrong from right? How do I make sure they have good values and treat others and themselves with respect?

"You love them," my parents said. "You stay involved with them. You give them your heart and your time."

In the beginning, though, that wasn't easy.

How could I be a hands-on dad when my hands were on a baseball bat in distant Montana?

The baseball bat, by the way, was wood, not metal. That was my first challenge. I'd played with metal bats my entire life. I was a bruiser with metal. Wood was new, and, to be honest, wood was scary. I started doing head trips on myself. *Maybe I'm a guy who can't hit with wood. Maybe the only reason I hit well in high school was because I have a feel for metal. Maybe there are guys who can hit only metal. Maybe some hitters are allergic to wood. Maybe I'll never be a good hitter again.*

I was tripping.

I was also thinking that I was a pitcher. I'd been drafted as a pitcher. In fact, Doc bought me shoes with pitcher's toes and an expensive pitcher's glove. I was known as Doc's nephew and I figured my future was in pitching. I figured wrong.

Milwaukee wanted me at shortstop.

I wanted to protest, but I also wanted to make good. After all, this is what I'd been living for. A shot at the majors. The big climb had begun and I was in no position to beef. So I sucked it up and played shortstop, all the while hearing Grandpa say, "A good player should be able to handle any position. Inside Power lets you do anything."

The Helena Gold Sox wore burgundy uniforms. Our socks were yellow and the stirrups—the socks worn outside the pants—were matching burgundy. Pretty sharp. Because Helena was such a tiny place with nothing happening, the Gold Sox were *it,* the city's only source of entertainment.

The loneliness got lonelier when I learned that we had to live in a dorm behind the ballpark. Four guys in a room. It was a dump. Thirty bucks a month.

I'd lie in bed at night remembering how excited I had been when I learned I'd been drafted. I dreamed of glamour and fame. And here I was in a sagging mattress infested with fleas and a dorm room that looked like a prison cell.

The wood bat issue played with my brain. The devil was telling me that my dream of a perfect family and perfect career was shattered. When I tried to hit, the bat gave me fits. The wood bat was vibrating and hurting my hands. My hands were getting sore; I was getting frustrated. I swung early and I swung late.

It wasn't the pitchers who were fooling me; I was fooling myself. Compared to the uncle who'd trained me, the pitchers weren't much. In fact, the stance I use today—where I wiggle my bat while waiting for the pitch—is something I developed to slow myself down. I also developed it because I wanted my own style. I stole part of that stance style from Joe Morgan, who'd cock his elbow like a chicken. I put the chicken and wiggle together and came up with something that suited me.

When I became a pro, I expected the pitchers to throw with a lot more heat. The wiggle was a way for me to hold back. Doc threw at 95 mph. These guys were lucky to reach 80. The fastball wasn't a problem, but I did have to learn to hit a breaking ball. It's good to have wrist speed—I always knew it was a huge advantage—but dealing with the subtleties of more specialized pitches took patience. And patience was something I lacked.

Although I felt like an outsider in Montana, I counted myself lucky to have a manager like Dave Huppert. He saw I was a fish out of water. He knew I was an only child away from home for the first time. He saw me calling my mom every night. I must have spent three thousand dollars a month on long distance. Huppert knew what I was going through.

On those ten-hour rides on the rickety bus all through Montana and Utah, the usual rule was that kids like me, just out of high school, had to sit in the back. The college grads sat up front. But Huppert sensed I was lonely and invited me to sit next to him. Little things like that made a world of difference. He also saw that I was tripping because of the wood bats. He could have blown a gasket and got on my case. But he didn't. He was understanding.

"Son," he said, "I see you're worried about these bats, but it's just a matter of time before you get used to them. Those

aluminum bats gave you an advantage. They drove the ball far-
ther. And now you feel like that advantage has been taken away.
The wood bat has a more legitimate speed. That's real bat
speed. The rhythm's different. But I've been watching you,
Gary, and I see you have a fine sense of timing. You feel the
rhythm of the game. Your instincts are right. It's just a question
of adjusting. That's what the rookie league is all about—taking
the time to make the adjustments. So take all the time you need.
You're going to do it, son, long as you relax."

When my manager talked that way, I was okay. Instead of
worrying about crushing the ball, I could look out the window
and see the beautiful mountains of Montana passing by. I could
see the blue sky and the puffy white clouds. I could relax.

It took a couple of weeks, but I finally made peace with the
wood. I started feeling the bat as an extension of my arms and
hands. I held it like it was mine. I held it like a weapon. And
somewhere in a rundown ballpark in the wilds of Montana, with
a couple of hundred people in the stands, I connected. Wood on
cowhide. That satisfying sound when the meat of the bat kisses
the pill right in the mouth. I watched it sail. When I got back to
the dugout, Huppert was smiling from ear to ear. He might have
been happier than me.

"Shef," he said, "you're going to be all right."

That year, during a very short season, I hit .365, fifteen home
runs, and seventy-one RBIs to lead the league.

Something else happened that year that was a thrill of a
lifetime.

I went to the World Series.

AMAZIN'

When I signed with the Brewers out of high school, I did something unusual during contract negotiations. I put in a deal breaker.

"The money's okay," I said, "but I want two first-class airplane tickets plus two tickets to this year's World Series."

The business guy from Milwaukee looked at me like I was nuts.

"No one's ever asked for anything like that before," he said.

"Well, first time for everything," I replied. "But I gotta have those tickets."

I got 'em. And my instincts proved right. In 1986, the Mets won 105 games. In the National League Championship Series against the Astros, Doc pitched great. In game 5, matched against

Nolan Ryan, he gave up only one run in eleven innings. Ryan did the same, but the Mets came through in the bottom of the twelfth. Game 6 went sixteen innings—New York 3, Houston 2—and, just like that, it was Mets vs. Boston in the World Series.

Best of all, I had my tickets. I took Linda. We joined Mom, Dad, Grandpa, and Grandma. It was a first for all of us. It was also my first taste of New York City championship baseball.

Dwight treated me great. He let me ride with the team. That was a team of rugged individualists and nonconformists. A quiet guy anyway, I was super quiet as I watched the players before the game. I didn't say a word to anyone, but my eyes were wide open and my mind was going crazy. I saw how the New York fans were also crazy—crazy enthusiastic, crazy critical, crazy intense. They were the craziest fans I'd ever encountered, and it made me think that one day I had to play on a New York team. When it comes to baseball, I decided, New York is the place.

When Doc pitched, I was more nervous than him. I was amazed to watch him face Don Baylor, Wade Boggs, Jim Rice. There was Roger Clemens. There was the Green Monster at Fenway Park, where the seats were set so crooked you had to sit sideways to see the game.

Doc didn't have a good series, but the Mets did. These were the Amazin' Mets who wouldn't go down for anyone. These were also the Red Sox still living under the 1918 curse and paying the price for trading the Babe to the Yankees. The curse hit Boston in Game 6 at Shea. They were up 3 games to 2. They were ahead 5–3 going into the bottom of the tenth when they retired the first two Mets. Only one out away from breaking the curse. Then came three straight singles. Mookie Wilson's grounder, an easy out up the first-base line, went through Bill Buckner's legs. Mets won. Series tied. Next day, Mets won the seventh game. Series over. Curse continued.

I watched it all like a cat studying goldfish. My concentration never wavered.

Someday I'll be here. I have to be here.

With that taste of New York City big-league energy strong in my soul, I felt recharged. I had to work my way out of the minors.

INTO THE MINORS

My ruthless pursuit of the majors was still the main focus. After my excellent rookie year, I thought I was ready. The Brewers didn't. The Brewers said I needed more time, so they sent me to Stockton, California.

The Brewers had a high A team and a low A team. Stockton was high A but Stockton still wasn't what I wanted. I was moving up, but not fast enough.

During the winter in Tampa, I spent time with my baby girls. As a seventeen-year-old father of two, I did the best I could, but my mind was always on baseball. I hated the idea of not having one simple happy family for my kids. Linda and I broke up; and of course, I'd long before broken up with Davine. I hated how I'd messed up my relationships so early on. But what could I do? There was no one to blame but myself.

When the season started and I went out to California—a big improvement over Montana—I tried to take out my frustrations on opposing pitchers. By then I felt more comfortable being away from home. I didn't have to call my mother five times a day. I got my own apartment. I learned to use a checking account and pay my own bills. I'd even started cooking my own food. Little by little, I was growing up.

But Stockton proved to be a crisis point. It wasn't my performance that caused the crisis; I continued to hit for a high average and field with the best of them. In my mind, the Stockton manager was the problem. The man had a trigger temper. When he didn't like something you did, he turned red and cursed like a sailor. I was used to Dave Huppert, who was sensitive and patient. This new guy was always flying into rages. I hated his style of managing.

At first I just let it go. My dad and granddad used to say, "Always listen to your manager. There can only be one boss on a team—and he's it. Learn to live with that." That was the creed I tried to follow. For the first few weeks in Stockton, when the manager went after me for some minor infraction, I sucked it up.

Then Mom and Dad came to Stockton to see me play. I was excited that they were in the stands. Whenever my family comes to watch me, I'm happy. Gives me extra motivation.

Around the third inning I'm at shortstop. Man at first. Line-drive double into right center. Runner rounds third and heads for home. Center fielder doesn't have a great arm and throws it to me, the cut-off man, on a bounce. The ball lands on a little drainage hole and takes a wild bounce. I can't get to it in time to throw out the runner. He scores. I'm given an error. That's crazy. That's wrong. I'm incensed. I throw down my glove in disgust and yell up at the scorer, "Are you blind?"

I try to settle down but I'm still worked up. Next batter hits a grounder right at me. I scoop it up and rocket it to first. I've always had a strong arm, but this time it's too strong. I throw the ball into the stands, not on purpose, but just because that unfair error has me off balance.

Manager loses it. Yells from the dugout, "Get in here, Sheffield, you're out of the game!"

He thinks the wild throw was intentional. He thinks he's going to embarrass me in front of my parents and the fans. But he's not. I'm not moving. I'm staying in the game.

"I said get in here!" he's screaming.

I don't budge. What's he going to do, run out on the field and drag me in?

When the inning's over and I get to the dugout, he calls me everything in the book. Never been cursed out like that before. I just sit there and take it, but when the game's over and my dad asks me what the manager said to me, I tell him.

Dad goes back to the manager's office.

Dad's there a long time.

When Dad emerges, he motions for me to come outside.

"Look, son," says my father when we're alone, "I've always told you to listen to your coaches. But you don't have to listen to anyone when they use profanity. I told the man that and he promises not to do it again."

I thought that was the end of the story—but it wasn't.

Dad's dressing down the manager made the guy even more resentful. He went out of his way to single me out for stupid infractions.

The straw that broke the camel's back had to do with socks and collared shirts. The manager had a rule: when we rode our raggedy bus we had to wear socks and collared shirts. Well, I'm from Tampa, where it's hot and all we wear is T-shirts. We never wear socks. Besides, when you're riding on the bus in the middle of hot and dusty California, why in the world should anyone care if you're wearing socks and collared shirts? It's not like *Gentlemen's Quarterly* magazine is photographing the team.

Anyway, the manager made the rule, but most of the guys ignored it. Me included.

Then one day we were getting on the bus to leave for a long road trip. I was in my seat when the manager came by and looked me over, like a sergeant inspecting his troops.

"No socks," he says. "No collared shirt. That'll be a two hundred dollar fine, Sheffield."

"That's ridiculous."

"What'd you say, Sheffield?"

"I said that's ridiculous. Half the guys on this team never wear collared shirts and socks and you don't say a word to them."

"Why don't you let me worry about enforcing my rules?"

"Why don't you leave me alone?"

"I won't tolerate back-talk."

"And I won't tolerate your dumb rules. You should be worried about how we play baseball, not what kind of shirts we're wearing."

With that, he lost it, cussing and calling me every name in the book.

I looked the man in the eye—looked at him real hard and long—and walked off the bus.

"Where you think you're going, Sheffield?" he yelled after me.

I didn't even bother to answer.

I was through

I was out of there.

I was quitting.

I couldn't stand this man, and I couldn't see myself playing another game for him.

When my teammates got to the next town, they called me and

said, "Gary, you can't quit. We need you. We'll talk to the manager and get him to call you. Work out your differences with him. Okay?"

"Okay," I agreed.

Half-hour later the phone rang. It was the manager, but before I could get a word out, he started up again, accusing me of undermining his authority and calling me a dirty this and dirty that.

I hung up on him.

I was ready to head home.

When I talked to Mama, she asked, "Are you sure you know what you're doing?"

When I talked to Daddy, he asked the same thing.

Word got to Doc, who was on the road with the Mets. He called right away. "You're going to throw away your whole career over nothing. Now get on the bus and join your team."

"I'm not doing it," I told my uncle.

"I'm telling you, Gary, do it."

I ignored him. But it was a lot harder to ignore my grandfather.

"Listen, son," he said, "I understand you. You're a fighter. No one's gonna insult you. No one's gonna run over you. You ain't made to be abused. All that's good. That's your character and that's your strength. But sometimes you gotta put your wisdom above your will. Your will is powerful, but wisdom should be more powerful. Wisdom asks you, 'What's your long-term goal here? What are you trying to achieve?' The answer's easy. The big leagues. You'll be there in no time. You keep this feud going with your manager and you'll be nowhere. Think about it, Bug."

I thought about it.

I caved in, got on a Greyhound, and joined the team.

CLOSING IN

A year in the minors can feel like ten. You're waiting and waiting. The waiting can drive you mad, especially if you're a cocky, lonely, determined teenager named Gary Sheffield.

I was seventeen years old and I didn't know anything, but I thought I knew a lot. The main thing I knew was that the minors were a stepping stone I wanted to step over as soon as possible. I didn't care what kind of punishment the majors might hold; I could take it. My entire childhood was a lesson in taking punishment from my uncle. I was trained to take whatever the big kids had to dish out. To face the big kids in the majors would be nothing new. From the first time I picked up a ball, the pattern had been the same: I had to prove myself.

I'd proven myself in Class A ball. I drove in 104 runs. My grandpa and daddy always said that the great players drive in at least 100 runs a year. I saw 100 as a benchmark. Since for the first time in my life I'd surpassed that magic number, I figured I was ready. Seemed that the Brewers felt the same, because that spring they sent me to big league camp.

My big test came when we played the Mariners in their park in Arizona. Mark Langston was pitching. I hadn't heard of him, but everyone said he was an ace. They said he threw blinding heat. They also said that just because I tore up the A league didn't mean I could deal with killer pitchers like Langston.

I remember Langston taking an awfully long time getting to the mound. I remember the tension building, and I remember feeling butterflies when I stepped into the batter's box. I also remember smashing his first pitch off the top of the wall for a stand-up double. Next trip to the plate I smacked a triple into deep right center. Third time up, line drive single up the middle. I ended the day a home run short of hitting for the cycle. My confidence shot up like a rocket.

Spring training just kept getting better. I led the team in all hitting stats. Then I heard that Brewers starting infielder Paul Molitor had broken his finger and I was tapped to replace him. First thing I did was call home.

"Mama!" I shouted, "I've made it. The Brewers called me up."

Mama called Daddy to the phone and Daddy called Grandpa and Grandpa called Doc and Doc called me and I couldn't sleep that night.

The dream was coming true.

Except it wasn't.

A week later word came down that Molitor was going to be okay after all. The Brewers didn't need an infielder.

Okay, I thought, *but at least they'll put me in Triple A.*

They put me in Double A. They shipped me out to El Paso.

.   .   .

El Paso was better than Helena and maybe even better than Stockton, but El Paso was still in the middle of nowhere.

Didn't matter. The Brewers owned the El Paso Diablos and I became a Diablo.

I made up my mind to adjust, and I did. I even drove my Corvette from Tampa. I was trying to feel at home.

My teammates had heard I'd enjoyed a hot spring training and wanted to see how I'd do against the best AA pitcher, Ramon Martinez, Pedro's older brother. Ramon was with San Antonio, a Dodger farm club.

Watching the guy warm up, I could see he was dynamite. Other than Doc, I'd never seen anyone throw that hard. He was fanning hitters left and right.

I went up there, eager to get in my licks. If I could hit Doc, I reasoned, I could hit Ramon. And I did. Drove one over the shortstop's head. While everyone was striking out, I was smoking the ball. Maybe El Paso wouldn't be so bad after all.

El Paso was cool except for one difficult day. The difficult day should have been a good day, because I hit a big home run. But one angry fan didn't see it that way.

El Paso has this tradition that after a Diablo hits a homer he goes along both dugouts, reaching into the stands with his helmet in hand so fans can drop in dollars. Later he gets two free pairs of Tony Lama boots.

Well, on this steamy Saturday afternoon I'd knocked one out of the park. The trouble was, though, by the time I'd finished getting high-fives from my teammates, the next batter had lined out to end the inning. There wasn't time to pass my helmet. I had to run out in the field. I thought the fans understood. And they did. Except for one.

At the end of the game, when I got to my Corvette, I stopped in my tracks. My car was trashed: windows smashed, doors kicked in, body keyed from front to back. I was enraged. I was ready to get out of El Paso and never come back. This was what you got for hitting a home run? I understood that traditions were important—and I respect traditions—but any fool could see I hadn't had time to honor the tradition.

Fortunately, Diablo management took care of fixing my car. I appreciated it. And I appreciated it when, halfway through the season, Brewers management moved me to Triple A to play with the Denver Zephyrs.

I was eager to get to Denver because the Zephyrs had a legendary player named LaVel Freeman. Freeman had hit .395 in Double A, and I wanted to see him in action. I've always been curious about—and eager to play with—legendary players, because they can teach me. Besides, I wanted to see if I could measure up.

LaVel was great. He'd always hit third, but when I joined the team they asked him whether he wanted to change his spot.

"Put me cleanup behind Gary," he said. "Gary's a guy who gets on base."

It was LaVel who first set me up as a number three hitter. His confidence in me meant a lot. He took me under his wing and never went anywhere without me. We became close. With LaVel, Billy Jo Robidoux, Brad Komminsk, and Steve Kiefer, we had an all-star team.

I also remember when Tito Landrum, a star with the great 1985 St. Louis Cardinals, came down to play in the league and gave us a taste of what superstars are all about. He was on that championship team with Joaquin Andujar, Ozzie Smith, Willie McGee, Jack Clark, and Terry Pendleton. Just being on the same field with Tito was a thrill.

The Denver experience was tremendous. That year I hit .327, connected for twenty-eight home runs, and drove in 119 runs. I'd proven myself and was ready to be called up. But the call never came.

To better my chances and stay in shape, I decided to go to the winter league. When I told management, they said no. Too big a danger of getting hurt. I told them it was my decision, not theirs. Their comeback was strong: "If we bring you to the majors as a September call-up, will you drop the idea of playing in winter league?"

Consider the idea dropped.

FOUR YEARS

When you look back at your life, four years doesn't seem like a long time. But when you're living your life, and you're still a teenager, four years is forever.

From ages nineteen to twenty-three I played infield for the Milwaukee Brewers.

I established myself as a major league player of quality, but I was never happy.

There are players who don't complain and can adjust to any situation. There are players who are silent in the face of what they consider wrong-headed management or unfair treatment. Sometimes these players are celebrated as heroes because they have a get-along, go-along attitude. You'll hear a baseball announcer say, "Everyone just loves this guy. Never beefs, never argues with anyone, he's a gem."

Well, maybe he is a gem. Or maybe he's scared.

For years, my uncle was described as a gem. He was Mr. Perfect as far as management went. He said what they wanted him to say. He became who they wanted him to be. He was groomed to be an all-American hero, a man loved by everyone. And he was. Because Doc was by nature nonconfrontational, he went along with their program. But he held his frustrations inside, which only led to greater frustrations.

The big shock about Doc came a year before my major league debut, during spring training in 1987. About the same time I learned that the Brewers were sending me to El Paso, I also learned, along with the rest of the sports world, that my uncle had tested positive for cocaine use. Instead of starting the season for the Mets, Dwight entered rehab.

My uncle is part of my life—he's my blood—and I've always felt connected to him. When his drug problem came out, I thought about him every day and every night. We talked. I didn't ask a lot of questions. I didn't pry. But I kept telling him that I was there for him. I still am. Family first. That's what Mama taught me; that's how Mama lived.

I knew my uncle liked to party, but I never knew exactly what the partying consisted of. He kept me away from that stuff. During the days when we spent so much time together, Dwight always protected me from what he considered negativity. I was curious and wanted to see where he was going; I wanted to know what he was doing, but Doc was firm. He never let me into that world. I figured that world wasn't about anything more than drinking and smoking. I didn't know about the coke.

I saw it like this: Dwight had a problem that he was taking care of. He'd come out of rehab and the problem would be gone. I didn't understand anything about addiction and how it destroys lives.

I did understand, though, that Doc had a problem expressing

what he really felt. He was the Golden Boy. He'd been groomed as the perfect player and the perfect guy. That wasn't real. That was public relations. No one's perfect, either as a player or as a person. We all have our dark sides, and we all have our beefs.

When we voice those beefs, we're given a bad rap. We're accused of being ungrateful; we're called difficult.

But from the get-go, it didn't matter to me how I was labeled. If I had a legitimate complaint, you'd hear about it. I didn't care about public relations. Didn't care about image or living up to someone else's notion of etiquette. I didn't care about any of that stuff.

My attitude was simple and unchangeable: I tell *my* truth. When something bothers me, I let you know. I can't be who you want me to be. I *won't* be who you want me to be. I have to be who I am.

I lived that first year in Milwaukee in a state of heightened emotion. I was determined. I was going to blast every pitch. I was going to show everyone what I was made of. I'd been preparing for this moment my whole life. I went out there with the conviction and confidence of a seasoned warrior.

And I stumbled.

Stumbled badly.

Stumbled so badly, in fact, that the fans booed.

That shocked me to the core of my soul. I'd never been booed before. Starting out in Little League, everyone in the stands always encouraged me. In my mind, I went back to Al Lopez Field in Tampa when Pete Rose had made an error. We fans had encouraged him. I thought baseball was all about encouragement. Man, those boos cut me to the core.

Of course I knew *why* they were booing. I wasn't performing. I was this hotshot kid fresh up from AAA, where I'd built a reputation as someone who could crush the ball. Everyone knew my uncle was Doc Gooden and everyone knew the Brewers had given me bonus-baby money because they thought I was a star. So how did I start off?

In a slump. And in a funk.

Maybe it was nerves, maybe it was not liking the cold climate. Maybe it was old-fashioned inexperience. Maybe it was just a teenager folding under pressure. Whatever it was, I sure wasn't easy on myself.

Bottom line: I was chasing bad balls and missing good ones. The more I floundered, the harder I was on myself. I'd always dreamed that my major league debut would be nothing short of spectacular. I never dreamed it would be spectacularly bad.

The truth is that I had a hard time getting over my first big league at-bat. It was against the Tigers on Sunday, September 4, 1988. I hammered a pitch down the left field line and into the stands. I watched it land fair. The ump called it foul. I wanted to argue but stopped myself. I wasn't going to win that argument. I felt even worse when the replay showed that the ball was clearly fair.

That started the slump.

Slumps feed on themselves. They work on your mind. They have you regretting the past and remembering all the at-bats you messed up. They have you fearing the future. *Will I ever get a hit again?* You're either behind yourself or ahead of yourself. You're never with yourself. You're never in the Now.

The Now is where you need to be.

The Now is the zone.

The Now isn't about what happened yesterday and the Now isn't what will happen tomorrow.

The Now is happening right in this instant.

The Now escaped me during those first weeks.

I couldn't buy a hit.

The boos, the fears, the negative voices inside my head pushed me out of the Now and had me flailing.

I went 0 for 4 during that first game. Then, in a two-game series against the White Sox in Chicago, I was 0 for 6.

When we came home to County Stadium, I found myself facing Mark Langston—the same Langston I'd hammered in training camp. I knew I could hit this guy. But my first at-bat wasn't pretty; he got me on a bad pitch.

My big league batting average remained .000.

When I came up in the sixth inning, the boo birds were on me. I tried not to hear, but, believe me, I heard. Tried to concentrate on nothing but Langston and his delivery. He came low and inside. That was all I needed. *Boom!* I sent it sailing over the left field fence. My first hit was a homer to tie the game at 1–1. Then, in the bottom of the eleventh, with Langston still on the mound, my second hit was a single to drive in the winning run.

I was sure I'd snapped the slump. But I hadn't.

The rest of September was rough. I was still struggling. The boos were back and the blues hit me hard. The batting coach was telling me to lose the wiggle and change my stance.

"Don't do it, Bug," said Grandpa when I called him. "That's your natural stance. You can't fool with what's natural. You'll come around. This is mental stuff, not physical. You need to deal with your mind. Best way to do that is just before you step up to the plate, imagine you're back in the Belmont Heights Little League. Imagine you're home."

Using that trick of imagination was easy when the Brewers went into Anaheim. The Angels had two pitchers—Rich Monteleone and Vance Lovelace—who came from Tampa. They're Doc's age, and back in the day Rich had competed against Dwight and Vance had been on Dwight's team.

Vance picked me up at my hotel. He knew I was having problems.

He said the same thing as Grandpa. "Just imagine you're back in Tampa. Hey, man, you're Doc's nephew. You're going to do just fine."

Even though he was on the opposing team, Vance treated me the way Doc did. I was his homeboy and he did everything he could to get me back in the groove.

With Tampa on my mind, with Tampa in my heart, during the next four games I went ten for eighteen and knocked in six runs.

It would have been a beautiful period except for one thing I hadn't counted on—one thing, in fact, I hadn't even known about: rookie hazing.

In a million years I never would have thought I'd submit to it. I submitted because I respect tradition. Tradition made me wear a woman's dress as I walked through a major airport from the curb all the way to the gate. The guys didn't pick out just any woman's dress for me. They picked out one that was especially tight. They wanted to make sure my big butt got lots of attention. Not only that, they made me wear pumps. I couldn't walk in the pumps, so they agreed I could wear sneakers. Imagine the sight: macho me sashaying down the corridors with everyone staring at me in my super-tight dress and tennis shoes. Bad enough that it happened once. But the team decided that tradition required I do it twice.

Everyone howled. I cringed.

Meanwhile, the end of my slump didn't mean the end of our team's struggle. The Brewers wound up tied for third place with Toronto in the Eastern Division, a game behind Detroit and two games behind first-place Boston.

In the twenty-four games I played that first year, I hit .238. Writers were saying that even though I could jump on inside fast-balls—my meat and potatoes—I was ineffective with curves and changeups that floated on the outside of the plate.

The writers weren't wrong.

I had work to do.

I worked hard that winter, got into a jogging routine and returned to spring training in great shape. Nothing was going to get in my way. Nineteen eighty-nine was going to be my year.

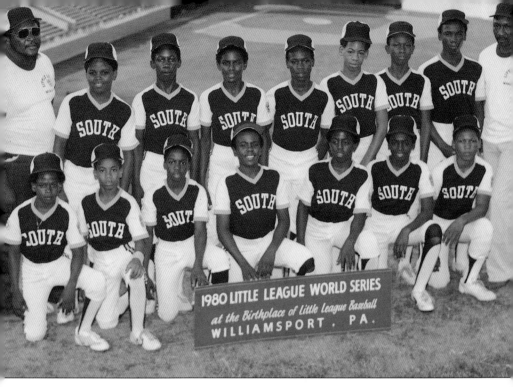

When I was eleven years old, my first Little League team made its way into the Little League World Series. When we lost, even the toughest of us cried our little eyes out. That's me in the front row, last on the right.

Me in my Little League uniform with Mom. In what turned out to be my first disagreement with "management," I argued with the coach and was kicked off the team. Sitting out the season felt like living in hell.

The next year, in the Belmont Heights Senior League, we finally triumphed. I pitched the world championship game, and we won hands down. I'm in the back row, all the way on the right.

That's me in seventh grade.

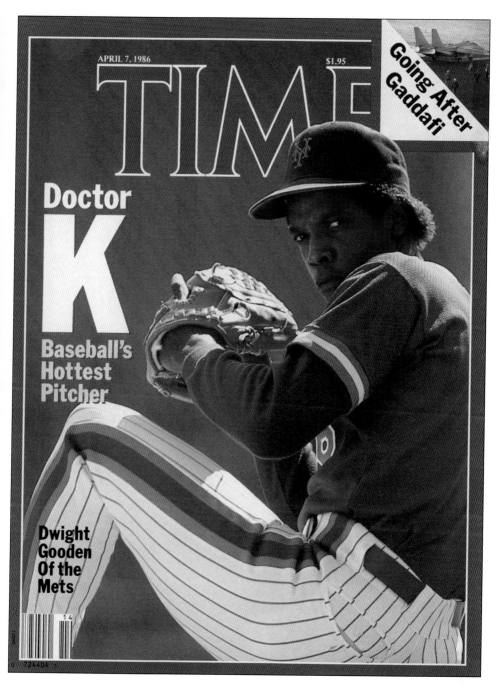

APRIL 7, 1986

$1.95

TIME

Going After
Gaddafi

Doctor
K
**Baseball's
Hottest
Pitcher**

**Dwight
Gooden
Of the
Mets**

In 1985, my junior year of high school, my uncle—and former backyard teammate—Dwight Gooden became a national sensation. But Doc never forgot me. He'd say, "I have this nephew down in Tampa who's going to be something." *Time & Life Pictures/Getty Images*

In 1987, I got drafted by the Milwaukee Brewers, one of Hank Aaron's old teams.

Opposite, top: Me and Doc in court in 1986, after a beating by police that caused the city of Tampa to explode. Eventually Dwight sued the police and won, but it was a reminder of how much racial healing is still needed. *AP/Joe Skipper*

Opposite, bottom: My grandfather, Dwight's dad, was the man who taught me about "Inside Power." His views on the indignities suffered by Hank Aaron strongly influenced the perspective I'd later bring to baseball.

Me as an El Paso Diablo, my third Minor League team. The Minors were rough for me. The waiting to get to "the show" can drive you mad.

Opposite: My mom, Betty, and my stepfather, Harold, who was really a dad to me growing up and who taught me valuable lessons about toughness.

There I am, nineteen years old, signing autographs before my first Major League game. *Tom DiPace*

With my new team, the San Diego Padres, I got to hit against Dwight for
the first time as a pro! Here we are together, hours before that game.
AP Photo/Richard Harbus

Opposite: I made my third All-Star game appearance in 1996 after a great
year; playing in 161 games, I wound up with 42 home runs, 120 RBI's, and
a batting average of .314. Meanwhile, the Marlins kept getting better.
Tom DiPace

In 1993, I was traded to my third team, the Florida Marlins—an expansion team in its first year of existence. I wasn't thrilled, but general manager Dave Domrowski told me, "In five years, Gary, you're going to lead us to a World Series." *Tom DiPace*

Going into 1997, the Marlins added manager Jim Leyland—the best moti-
vator I know—along with such players as Moises Alou, Bobby Bonilla, and
Alex Fernandez. Finally, we were ready. *Robert Mayer/ South Florida Sun-
Sentinel*

Opposite, top: In the Marlins' great 1997 post-season run, we were up
against Barry Bonds' Giants in the divisional series. This is me being
mobbed by my teammates after I'd slid home ahead of the tag to win the
second game. *AP Photo/Marta Lavandier*

Opposite, bottom: The World Series against the Indians was a classic, going
to extra innings in the seventh game. The intensity level was like nothing
I've ever experienced before. It was all such a rush. And, yet, the parties left
me feeling empty. I decided that night that something was missing from my
life. *AP Photo/Rogelio Solis*

This picture was taken the weekend I first met my future wife, DeLeon. We'd only spoken for an hour when I told her, "I'm going to marry you. You're going to be my wife."

It took a while, but I finally got D to marry me. Until DeLeon, my view of women was immature. It was street. D changed my attitude about women and a lot of things. I could feel my heart changing and expanding.

Opposite: After we won the World Series, I thought for sure the '97 Marlins team would be back together the next season to compete again. Instead, out of the blue, I was traded to the Dodgers. I ended up having three great years with the Dodgers—in large part because D was there with me.

The Atlanta Braves was the fifth team I played for. Atlanta was the first place where I could stop and appreciate what counted most: a loving wife, wonderful children, and that calmness that comes with faith. Also, I was reunited with Terry Pendleton, the man who'd first helped me spiritually when we were with the Marlins, and who was now the Braves' batting coach. *Reuters/Corbis*

I negotiated my Yankees contract myself with George Steinbrenner. Even with the help of Doc (right), the negotiations were rough. I walked out on George multiple times, and some of our disagreements continued to fester through the years I was putting up MVP caliber numbers in pinstripes. *Getty Images*

Me warming up with A-Rod and Jeter, two players I have immense respect for, not least because of how they handle the pressure on them.
Tom DiPace

Shef's Chefs made an appearance at Yankee stadium in 2004. I first noticed this phenomenon when playing for the Braves. The hat-wearing fans would yell, "You're our man, Shef. You're the one, baby." I found myself getting all choked up. *Getty Images*

In 2004, I was going after a line-drive at Fenway Park when a fan took a swipe at me and actually smacked me in the face. In my younger days, I would have hit back hard, but I'd finally found the calmness to not respond that way. *Getty Images*

In the Series-clinching game of the 2004 Division Playoffs, I was at bat in the eleventh inning when A-Rod stole home on a wild pitch, and the Series was ours! *AP Photo/Chad Rachman*

But 1989 wasn't my year. If anything, it was the most difficult year of my professional life.

Big league pitchers continued to baffle me—two in particular.

The first was Dave Stewart. Nothing had prepared me for Stewart, not even Doc. I caught up with Dave at the peak of his career, during those four years when he won twenty games or more. He was the backbone of that Oakland team that included Ricky Henderson, Mark McGwire, and Jose Canseco.

Stewart had this aura about him.

First off, he was big and used his size to his advantage. He pulled his cap over his eyes until you couldn't get a glimpse of his face. And then he worked fast. He took care of you in no time. He pitched effortlessly. He treated you like you weren't a threat, just a nuisance. Boom-bang, you were gone. Stewart had my number. I couldn't get a hit off him. When we went to Oakland, and when Oakland came to Milwaukee, I knew another test was coming at me. All year I flunked. It wasn't until May of 1990, my third year in the majors, that I managed a hit off Stewart. I felt like I'd broken a sorcerer's spell.

The other pitcher who gave me fits was Nolan Ryan. Ryan didn't have the mysterious hide-your-eyes-under-your-cap vibe of Stewart. He had something else: He'd scare you out of your wits. He'd throw at your head. He'd throw in front of you, and then he'd throw in back of you. You felt a murderous intent.

Now, intimidation is part of the game; always will be. I don't mind intimidators. Usually they just get my juices flowing. But Nolan was something else. He didn't think twice about knocking you down. You'd get up and he'd knock you down again. I had visions of one of his fireballs ripping off the side of my head. It wasn't the pain I was worried about; it was a supersonic bean ball that would end my career.

When I started out, I was unhappy with the Brewers pitching staff over the issue of retaliation. I was getting more than my fair share of bean balls. As a former pitcher, I figured that you give as good as you get. That's how I learned the game: If a pitcher throws at you, next inning your guy throws at them. You retaliate. Yet our pitchers weren't doing that.

I kept that feeling in for a long time, but it kept gnawing at me. A reporter who covered the team was talking to me one day after a game when I'd been knocked down twice by pitchers. The writer asked me how I felt about it. "Isn't anything I'd want written about," I said, "but it ticks me off that our pitchers don't back me up by backing them down." I went on about how I wasn't being supported by my colleagues. When Paul Molitor, my teammate and a big star, was knocked down, the pitching staff always retaliated. When I was knocked down, that was the end of it. I was mad, and it felt good to finally tell someone my true feelings.

It didn't feel good, though, to read my statements, exaggerated to sound more dramatic, in the newspaper the next day. Reporters need stories and will do anything to create controversy. Back then I didn't understand that. In my naive way, I thought I was speaking in confidence. Man, it was a rude awakening.

My teammates were angry. Management was angry. But when they asked me about my statements, I couldn't lie. "I didn't want it in the paper," I said, "but that's how I feel."

And, by the way, my feelings on that subject haven't changed.

The other big issue was who'd play shortstop, me or Billy Spiers. Spiers had been brought to the Brewers after a very short time in AA. I'd paid my dues in rookie ball, A, AA and AAA. In that short September stint in 1988—just twenty-four games—I drove in twelve runs, scored twelve times and hit four homers—and that was batting at the end of the order. Before that I had torn up the minors, hitting fifty home runs in AA and AAA combined. Plus, my fielding was good. I'd committed very few errors. Spiers' numbers didn't come close to mine. I remember the compliments I got from management the first time I faced Roger Clemens and went three for three.

Now suddenly management was pitting me against Spiers for a position I figured was rightfully mine. I was also told to prepare as a backup third baseman. Well, I didn't want to play third. Paul Molitor was at third, no easy man to replace.

I didn't blame my manager for this. I loved Tom Trebelhorn. He was like a father. Tom had the patience and personality of a good schoolteacher. The man had no ego. He also had no real power. Power stayed in the hands of Bud Selig.

When it came to business, Bud was sharp as a tack. He was also a shark. But we had a good relationship. In the beginning, before I understood how business ruled the game, I was just a guy observing the scene. Bud was cool with me; I was cool with him.

At the same time, I let people know how I felt about the shortstop controversy. I also couldn't help wondering if there'd even *be* any competition were the color reversed—that is, if Spiers were black. In my mind, I was convinced a white Gary Sheffield would have been handed the job, no questions asked.

The bigger issue was that I never felt accepted by the Brewers. The vibe wasn't right—not from my teammates and not from management.

The breaking point, literally, came early in 1989. It had to do with a break in my foot. It might sound like a small incident, but when I look back, I see it as the turning point, the single incident that ended my innocence and, for the rest of my life, changed my attitude about baseball.

I'd never think about the game the same way again.

THE BREAK

Despite my feelings about the Brewers, the front office wanted me to know that they believed in my future. Selig kept telling me that he had faith in my ability.

"Fine," I said, "but actions speak louder than words."

Bud took action. He put a $7 million deal on the table.

I was impressed.

Then in the first half of the 1989 season, in a game against the Royals, I pounded what looked like a stand-up double into left field. But Bo Jackson fielded it perfectly and, as I was rounding first, he threw an unbelievable strike to second base. I had to stop in my tracks and hustle back to first. When I slammed on the breaks, a spike got caught on the carpet and I jammed my foot something fierce. I thought I felt something tear, but shook it off and played hurt.

The trainer looked at it and said it was nothing. I kept playing. Every time I went to my right to plant my foot, though, I'd fall down. And the pain didn't diminish. I went back to the team doctors, who said it was just a question of time before it healed.

Meanwhile, though, my performance suffered. It suffered so bad that the Brewers decided to send me down to the minors. I was incensed.

"That's crazy," I said. "It's my foot. Something's wrong with my foot."

My protests did no good. When I arrived back in AAA, my foot felt even worse. Rather than risk a career-ending injury, I refused to play.

The minor league manager got on me.

The minor league players got on me.

One guy cornered me in the locker room and said, "What's wrong, Sheffield, you think you're too good to play with us? I think you're scared you'll mess up here and get sent back to rookie ball."

Rather than answer him, I shoved him so hard he flew across the room. When he came at me, I was ready. Nothing would have pleased me more than to have knocked his block off. But the other players separated us.

The other players adopted his attitude: Why is Sheffield sitting on the bench? If he was sent down to help this team, why isn't he helping? We have to obey orders. Why doesn't he?

I kept hearing those voices, but those voices didn't matter. The voice that mattered was the voice of reason. That voice said, "See your own doctor." I did.

He said my foot was fractured. I wasn't surprised. I'd figured it was broken. That was why I couldn't find my balance. That was why the pain was extreme.

Rather than deal with Brewers management, I filed a petition through the Players Association, claiming I'd been sent down to the minors unjustifiably. My doctor's report gave me an ironclad case.

I won. I was sent back to Milwaukee. Eventually my foot was set in a cast, forcing me to sit out the rest of the season. Management apologized. They wanted me to know they'd made a mistake. But to me the apology didn't mean anything.

It wasn't that I don't believe in forgive-and-forget; I do. But during this drawn-out injury episode, Bud Selig took his $7 million offer off the table. He admitted their medical mistake, but that didn't change the fact that I was now an unknown quantity. And he wasn't about to risk any more money on me.

Suddenly my eyes opened. Suddenly I saw the baseball world the way it really is:

Business rules.

Money rules.

You can love a player's ability. You can promise him the moon. You can tell him that the future is his, that he hasn't joined a team, he's joined a family. You can tell him that the family comes first. Doesn't matter what you tell him. The minute the player looks like a bad investment, you forget your promise and consult your lawyers. You run to protect your financial stake. The player is no different than a piece of real estate or a prize bull. He represents nothing but a return on your investment.

I was twenty before I learned this hard lesson. It wasn't that others hadn't warned me; Daddy and Grandpa had told me that pro baseball was a cold-blooded business. Grandpa had said that baseball can break your heart. But I had to live through it myself, see it with my own eyes, experience it firsthand.

Reality slapping you across the face sure does sting.

I felt abandoned and I felt lonely, as lonely as when I'd played for Helena.

I wanted to say to Selig, *"I'm gonna heal; I'm gonna dominate this league; I'm gonna be a great hitter and a great fielder;*

I'm going to play in All-Star games and help teams win champi-onships; I'm going to be good not for five years, but ten years, fifteen years, twenty years. Don't give up on me now. Put that offer back on the table. Believe in me."

But I didn't say a word.

I knew it'd do no good.

Selig had made up his mind.

This was the way of the world.

Okay, world, I said to myself, *if baseball is all about business, then I'm going to be a businessman. I'm going to treat this game the way they do. At every critical turn, I'm going to ask myself the questions:*

How can I maximize my revenue?

How can I increase my worth?

A MAN AMONG MEN

I was at my parents' home in Tampa. My daughter Ebony was in her high chair, Mom was fixing lunch, and Dad was off at work. The call came in December.

"Gary, this is Don Baylor, and I'm calling to let you know that the Brewers are thinking of hiring me as a batting coach."

"I hope that happens, Don," I said. "I'd love it, man."

Baylor had been a batting star over the course of a nineteen-year career. He'd played with everyone from the Orioles to the Yankees to the Red Sox. I really respected the guy.

"The reason they're talking to me, Gary, has a lot to do with you. They want you to know they care about you. They want to give you a coach you can be comfortable with. But to be honest, Gary, I'm not worried about what they think. All I know is that you've got a great future and if I can help you, I will."

90

"I appreciate that, Don."

A week later he called to say that his job had come through.

"We're going to have fun, Gary, and we're going to work hard. So forget about everything that's happened before. We're only going to think about what's happening now. I guarantee you, you're going to have a good year."

That's Don Baylor, a man among men.

When I got to spring training, Don was there with a video cassette player. He was among the first guys to use them. He had every opposing pitcher on tape and would sit me down next to him as he explained their moves.

"You're impatient, Gary. You're swinging too quickly and too often. Make these guys work harder. Take them deep into the count. Feel 'em out. Wait 'em out. Patience is a hitter's best friend."

Don became a dad and, believe me, all baseball players—especially the young ones—need to have dads around. Don also had a work ethic as strong as mine. And he was all about practice.

One day he was throwing batting practice, schooling me in hitting to the opposite field. I mistakenly hit one back to the mound that struck Don square on the nose. I hit the thing hard. I was scared he'd be angry. But he wasn't. He shook it off like it was nothing. Later we went into the dugout, where the trainer saw that his nose was broken. Don still wasn't mad.

"Let's get back out there," he said, not raising his voice. "I'll keep pitching and you keep driving it to right."

"Don't you think you should go tend to your nose?"

"Later, Shef," said Baylor. "We got work to do first."

And for another hour he kept pitching while I kept hitting. Don was the guy who taught me to hit to the opposite field.

The other great addition to the 1990 Brewers—a team already strong in talent with Robin Yount, Paul Molitor, Glenn

Braggs, Teddy Higuera and Don August—was Dave Parker as designated hitter. Dave was the man.

When he was with the Reds and I was still in school in Tampa, I'd go to Al Lopez Field and watch Dave run hundreds of sprints with his earphones on. He never tired and his spirit never weakened. He was one of my idols. He was also Mr. Personality and Mr. Prankster. Everyone loved him. When they told me I'd be batting third and he'd be hitting cleanup, I felt secure. Dave Parker had my back.

The season started slowly. I didn't homer all of April. On May 1 we were in Kansas City facing Royals ace Bret Saberhagen. First two times up, he struck me out. After the second time, Don said, "Come back to the locker room for a quick minute." He had those strikeouts on tape so he could show how my feet were set awkwardly. In the sixth inning, when I faced Saberhagen for the third time, I corrected my stance and blasted one into the seats. If I was a believer in Don's lessons before, I was a *true* believer now.

I also believed Don when he said to me, "Gary, I know you get ticked off when they throw at your head. Everyone does. But stop worrying about the retaliation. Leave that up to us."

Week or so later—I think it was in Detroit—a pitcher almost took my head off with a high fastball. I lost it; I started out for the mound. Both dugouts emptied out, with Don Baylor and Dave Parker leading the charge. After some serious shoving, calm was restored. I drew a walk and eventually scored. When I got back to the dugout, Don was waiting for me.

"Look, Gary," he said, "if I ever have to run out there again because some pitcher is buzzing you, you'd better deck the guy before I get to the mound."

"Yes, sir," I replied.

I liked this man's style.

Parker's style was also super-cool. I called him "Gentle Giant." He called me "Homeplate Face." He called Robin Yount

"General Custard." He called Paul Molitor "The Smartest White Man in the World" and always added, "but I'd never let you date my daughter."

The year ended disappointingly for the Brewers. Injuries plagued us and we wound up 74–88. The good news was that Robin Yount was voted MVP and Parker and I hit well. I had the highest batting average on the team—.294—with Dave close behind. I hit ten home runs, Dave hit twenty-one; I drove in sixty-seven runs, Dave drove in ninety-two. We fed off each other's energy, and I felt that I'd finally turned in a top-notch major league performance.

Maybe that's one of the reasons I was still miffed that they kept Spiers at shortstop and me at third. My attitude hadn't changed: I'd *earned* that position. If the press asked me about it, I told them just how I felt. When a reporter wondered whether I thought the decision had racial overtones, I wasn't about to lie. The white man was given preference, and that was that.

Management asked me to tone down my remarks. I refused. Harry Dalton, general manager, made many decisions I didn't like. When I expressed my opinions, I was accused of being disloyal. I called it being honest. When Dalton suffered a heart attack, I was accused of causing it. I was deeply sorry for the man's medical condition—fortunately, he recovered—but I didn't feel responsible. I don't respond to guilt-laying, which was what some people were putting on me.

My story in Milwaukee turned from bad to good, then back to bad and from bad to worse.

In 1992, they traded Dave Parker to the Angels. That broke my heart. Don Baylor also didn't stay long. Those guys guided me through my tough times in Milwaukee. They were the ultimate professionals. They were also a combination of brother and father. My baseball life was different without them.

"Baseball will break your heart." Grandpa's famous words.

The way he said those words, you knew he meant them. He'd lived them. Baseball's vicious racism had broken his heart. So had injuries.

Heartbreak is part of every player's life, whether he admits it or not. Losing Don and Dave devastated me. From what I could see, white players got preferential treatment, and it made me angry. And, as Grandpa and I had both learned, the likelihood of injuries made a fantasy of a smooth career where the trajectory goes up, up, up.

In 1992, I was down, down, down. I messed up my wrist, then my thumb, then my shoulder. Management tried to play down my injuries. In essence, they were telling me to play hurt. If I didn't, I'd be accused of disloyalty. The accusations flew, but I held my ground. I had a career to protect. I made a business decision. I wouldn't play until I healed. My season was over in July. That year I batted only 175 times. My average was the worst of my life, a pathetic .194.

I've never been more miserable.

Milwaukee wasn't my kind of town. Milwaukee wasn't my kind of team.

Far as I was concerned, Milwaukee was hell.

And then, just like that, it all changed.

In one fell swoop, I left hell with a one-way ticket to heaven.

THE HALLELUJAH
YEAR

t began with a ride in a white Porsche owned by San Diego
Padre Benito Santiago. Benito was something else.

Benito took me under his wing. When it was time to leave
training camp in Peoria, Arizona, Benito said, "Let's drive to San
Diego, bro. Let's put the top down and fly over to California in the
Porsche."

Blue sky, cool breezes, clear highways ahead.

It was the drive of a lifetime.

I had a new attitude. I had a new vision. Suddenly I saw the
world moving in slow motion. As I stood at home plate in Jack
Murphy Stadium in San Diego, I watched the ball leave the
pitcher's hand. The pitcher was moving in slow motion; the ball
was coming at me in slow motion; I could see the ball's seams

spinning slowly; I knew when to start my swing, when to lower or raise my bat, where to hit the ball.

My rhythms were right. I was kicked back, a beat behind my normal pace. And suddenly that backbeat gave me a leg up. I was right on time. Never rushing, never dragging, but smack in the middle of a mellow groove that never seemed to stop. The groove went on all year. Slow, steady, satisfying, absolutely beautiful.

San Diego was absolutely beautiful. I loved the fans, loved the weather, loved my teammates and my manager. I just loved being alive.

Happiness leads to happy results. I was like a man let out of prison. Every day was a gift, every chance to hit an opportunity to say thank you to the team that had plucked me out of hell.

San Diego general manager Joe McIlvaine said he'd called the Brewers at least two dozen times trying to get me. He was a believer. So was manager Greg Riddoch. Best of all were the other Padres.

Fred McGriff, a slugger from Tampa, was my uncle's age. Fred was a big brother. Nothing made me more comfortable than a brother from back home. Tony Fernandez and Benito were great. And of course Tony Gwynn, one of the best hitters in history, was a superstar.

"Welcome to the major leagues," Gwynn told me the day I arrived.

National Leaguers considered their league the best, the one where strategy mattered, not just brute force. National Leaguers thought they played baseball with more finesse than the American League. My uncle had that attitude, and I quickly adopted it myself. You'd hear National Leaguers say, "They don't have guys over here throwing 3-2 curveballs and bouncing 3-2 pitches. Brother, this league is serious."

One of my first thoughts when I went to the Padres was that I'd be facing my uncle. I looked on the schedule and saw we'd be playing the Mets in May. That was going to be something.

Meanwhile, I started off strong in April. Hitting between McGriff and Gwynn was a dream come true. Talk about security! My swing felt good, my legs were strong, I was fielding well at third and throwing to first with dead accuracy. Last year's injuries were a thing of the past.

The media started to build up the confrontation with Doc. Doc played it up. He told reporters he'd humiliate me by striking me out every time. He also said he'd hit a triple so he could stand at third and laugh in my face.

"I'm just bringing attention to you," said Dwight when he called. "You'll get a lot of good press out of this."

He was right. Every chance Doc had, he'd mention me to reporters. He'd been that way ever since I'd proven myself in Little League. "If you think *I'm* something," he'd say, "wait till you see my nephew."

The closer we got to the game, the more I thought about it. The truth was that Doc *did* want to strike me out, and I *did* want to take him deep. It'd been that way since we were kids, so why should it be any different now? We were blood, but we were competitors.

Even stronger than those competitive forces, though, were the memories. The memories were deep. As the team left on our road trip and began making our way to New York, I kept thinking about facing Doc. I thought about it in St. Louis and in Montreal. And when we got to Philly, just down the road from New York, I kept reliving those childhood scenes: Eight-year-old Bug trying to catch twelve-year-old Dwight, Bug running behind Dwight and Dwight's friends, Bug tagging along, Bug trying to catch up with the big boys.

Coming into New York City, seeing those skyscrapers, I realized that I *had* caught up. It was amazing, but my uncle and I were now major leaguers. We'd gone from the sandlots of Tampa to Shea Stadium, where it seemed a hundred photographers were taking our pictures.

"How does it feel, Gary," a reporter yelled out, "to be facing your uncle?"

"Feels great," I said. "I'm just blessed to be here."

The bigger blessing was that Dan Edward Gooden was sitting in the stands, beaming with pride. Whatever happened in the field, Grandpa was the winner, the inspiration, the man who'd gotten us there. Grandma, Mom, and Dad were sitting right next to him. Blessings everywhere.

As I crouched in the on-deck circle watching Doc pitch and waiting my turn, my mind was still in the past. I remembered the days when Dwight was pitching and, no matter how hot it was in the house, the air conditioning was off and the heater was on. Doc had a jacket wrapped around his arm. Grandpa insisted that he keep his arm warm. We'd sweat for hours so Doc could have a good day on the mound.

Now, coming to bat against him, I didn't want him to have a good day on the mound. I wanted for him to have a lousy day. I wanted my team to send him to the showers in the first inning. But the truth is that I was so nervous I was a little sick. After all, this wasn't just my uncle I was facing; this was the great Doc Gooden. My head was going crazy and, rather than keep my cool, I swung at anything. I was lucky to ground out to second. Least I didn't strike out.

In three confrontations I managed a single. The single felt like a grand slam. The bottom line is that I didn't humiliate myself. I stood up against Doc and didn't collapse. He never did strike me out. Doc and the Mets won the game 7–3, and we all walked away proud. When the ordeal was over, the family had dinner together in New York City.

This was Doc's eighth year in the majors, and he was still struggling. It had been four years since he'd been in an All-Star Game and he'd never quite regained that incredible form that had made him Rookie of the Year and a Cy Young Award winner. At the same time, my uncle wasn't about to quit. I could sense that his feelings were all bottled up inside. But I also knew he wasn't the type who wanted to talk about them.

Meanwhile, my family was—and is—devoted to Dwight. He returned that devotion the minute he made big money in baseball by buying beautiful houses for each of his two sisters, his parents, and himself on the same street in St. Petersburg. Doc wanted us all right next to each other.

As the season deepened, I still saw the pitches in slow motion. I had never hit so well in my life. That I was playing not only against my uncle, but also against guys like Darryl Strawberry and Eric Davis, was a constant thrill. Even more amazing was that I was outhitting them. When I got up in the morning, I had to pinch myself to make sure I wasn't dreaming.

I'd like to tell you that my amazing season came from super-strict training and good nutrition. Except it didn't. Great as he was, Tony Gwynn wasn't a weight lifter. Neither was Fred McGriff. Neither was I. I'd watch Tony eat a greasy meal just before the game and go out and hammer four hits. Fred could down three Snickers bars just before tearing up any pitcher in the league. I couldn't do that. But I could follow Fred's lead by working out on the bike before I left the locker room. That loosened me up. That was about it, though. It would make sense that my best year in the majors would be accompanied by intelligent and conscientious training. But it didn't happen that way. Out of instinct, out of deep relaxation, out of good feeling and good timing, out of this slow motion magic I was hitting the ball practically where I wanted, day after day.

It also helped that Greg Riddoch never pushed me. Riddoch was a laid-back manager who understood how pressure can hurt as much as help.

"We don't expect big numbers out of you, Gary, we just want you to relax."

Relaxation led to big numbers. By the end of June, they were calling the lineup of Tony Fernandez, Gwynn, Sheffield, and McGriff "The Four Tops."

As opposed to many Milwaukee fans, Padres fans were completely supportive. If I made an error at third, they'd shout, "Bad hop, Shef, you'll get it next time." Turned out I made only sixteen errors all year. I thought I might win a Gold Glove but Ken Caminiti, third baseman with the Astros, beat me out with eleven errors.

The 1992 All-Star Game was held in San Diego. When I was introduced during the home run–hitting contest, the ovation sounded like thunder. I'd never had an ovation like that before. Those fans warmed my heart.

Something else happened during the game that warmed my heart. Terry Pendleton got the start while I waited on the bench. But after his first at-bat he came back to the dugout and told the manager, "Take me out and put Gary in. This is his town, and they love him." That's about the classiest gesture I'd ever witnessed from another player. The manager put me in, and the crowd greeted me with love.

My love affairs were not restricted to the field. My good year, my coming of age as a major leaguer, and my recognition as a legitimate star jacked up my ego. I was flying high. Seems like confidence, cockiness, and ego are all part of the same attitude.

My attitude with women was: I'm single, I'm free, I'm willing if you are. Since my early dream of one woman/one life/one family had long been shattered, I was operating on the get-what-I-can principle. In fact, I became something of a magnet. I was always with a group of women. Teammates counted on me to hook them up. I liked that role. It increased my status and made me the key man in a critical area. Gary became the go-to guy.

I didn't have a steady and wasn't about to commit or propose to anyone. But an especially beautiful woman named Lori became a close friend. Lori lived in San Diego, and she had me loving the city even more.

Second half of the season I was on fire. The team cooled down and we weren't in contention, but I was contending for the Triple Crown and MVP. The fun part was that Fred McGriff and I were neck and neck; fans held up signs showing our closer-than-close stats. As we were heading for the finish line, I hurt a finger and fell into a little slump. That kept me from the Triple Crown and the MVP—won that year by Barry Bonds on the Pirates—but I won the National League batting championship at .330. Fred won the home run crown—thirty-five to my thirty-three—and I had 100 RBIs as opposed to his 104. Despite my long ball success, I struck out only forty times.

We wound up a couple of games above five hundred, but I personally felt over the moon. I never wanted to leave San Diego. I'd finally found a club to love for a lifetime. What Hank Aaron was to the Braves, I'd be to the Padres. Everything had fallen in place. Everything was the way I wanted it.

And things got even better when word came that Derek Bell, my homeboy from Tampa and Little League teammate, was joining the Padres. Nothing could have made me happier. A good team was now going to be a great team. If McGriff and I worked together like clockwork, Derek and I had even better rapport. Derek was family, Derek was home, Derek was proof that things had permanently turned around. After suffering through the cynicism and heartbreak of cold-blooded Milwaukee, the warm Southern California sun was shining on us all.

Life was beautiful. Life was sweet. Life was getting better every day.

THE GAME

The game can fool you. Just when you think it's all about money, you start forgetting about money and loving the game that you learned when you were a kid. That's what happened in San Diego.

Sure, Selig took my deal off the table when I got hurt; sure, that hardened me to the reality of cold-business baseball. But then, just like that, San Diego warmed me up. With Derek Bell part of my posse, I couldn't have been happier. I was playing the game because I loved the game. My little-boy love of baseball was back.

I'm not saying I forgot about money. But I didn't fight about money. The Padres offered me a $3.1 million deal that I accepted, no questions asked. I had no plans of going anywhere else.

I'd developed some style on the field—and off the field as well. Deion Sanders helped me. I always liked how Deion had a look. "Look, here, bro," he said, "you're a star, and it's time to look like one." Deion hooked me up with a custom tailor and custom jeweler. Here I was, a kid from Tampa who'd lived in T-shirts and sneakers, suddenly getting into cashmere and silk.

"Don't forget the watch," Deion said. "The watch makes the outfit."

The watch was a gold Rolex. The one I liked cost five thousand dollars. I studied that baby but couldn't get myself to buy it. Until then, the most expensive watch I'd owned had cost $49.95. Not long before that, I'd been buying only five dollars worth of gas for my Corvette, because five dollars was all I had. Spending five thousand for something to tell time seemed crazy.

I decided against it. But that night, I couldn't sleep. I kept seeing the Rolex flashing on my wrist. Next day I got up early, went to the man, and wrote out a check for five thousand dollars. Style didn't come cheap, but I decided I liked style.

I told you that Eric Davis had great style in clothes. Well, I was determined to develop my own style. I might have been the first player to tuck my pants inside my shoes. Then Nike wanted me to wear their high-tops, but I had them customize a three-quarter shoe. That started another trend.

Style is cool.

TV is cool.

I like watching TV comedies. And I was aware that Tom Werner had bought the Padres with the money he'd made on TV sitcoms. But I didn't really pay too much attention to the San Diego owner; I was too busy making my name and falling in love with the game all over again. As it turned out, Werner might have known how to run a TV empire, but he sure didn't know how to run a baseball team.

It was great that he traded for Derek Bell in 1993, and I loved having my homeboy on the Padres with me, but that season got off to a slow start. Attendance fell and Tom Werner freaked. Before mid-season, word came down that he'd fallen into a money crunch and had decided to sell off assets. People were calling it a fire sale. And of course, we were the merchandise, the products that had to go.

The result of all this?

Heartbreak.

"Baseball," said Grandpa, "will break your heart."

It happened so fast it had my head spinning.

One day San Diego was the Garden of Eden. Next day I was being kicked out of the Garden. And the reason? Not because I'd disobeyed, but just the opposite: I was being kicked out because I'd done so well. I was worth so much.

That recently renewed little-boy love of baseball turned back to disillusionment. The wakeup call was back.

"It's a business, boy," my father said when he heard the news. "You can't get away from business."

In a business, owners are entitled to make money. They *must* make money. I realized that early on. But with Tom Werner, I also saw how rich businessmen like to toy with baseball teams because they're a little-boy fantasy. Just as some boys dream of playing baseball, others—or grown men—dream of owning a team. That way they get to make *all* the decisions. Owners, like players, want to have fun.

But the difference is this: players have to really know how to play. They train. They develop. They come up through the ranks. They're tested every step of the way; they're tested every day.

Owners aren't tested. They don't have to know anything. They just need money. Money is their only requirement. With money, they get to decide the fates of dozens of lives: *you* stay here; *you* go there; I'm making *you* rich; I'm putting *you* out to pasture.

Players' fates are in the hands of owners. Some of those owners are experienced and wise. Others are inexperienced and stupid.

As a player, you roll the dice. You hope for a good roll. You hope for an owner who understands the nuances of this complicated game; you hope for an owner who has heart, who understands that he's dealing with human lives and not simply assets on a balance sheet. You hope he has soul.

If he doesn't, it doesn't matter.

You go where you have to go.

You do what you have to do.

You play the game.

HOME

I love Florida.

Florida is home.

Florida is where I learned my craft.

I like the weather, the people, the food. So why wasn't I thrilled when I learned I was being traded to the Florida Marlins?

Mainly because Florida was an expansion team in its first year. They weren't contenders. They were building a team, and that takes years. I wanted to be with a winner, right here, right now.

Going back to Florida also reminded me that my dream of domestic happiness wasn't happening. What was happening was that Lori, my friend in San Diego, became pregnant. Our son, Gary, Jr., was born in 1993, the same year I went to the Marlins. He was—and is—a blessing in my life and his mother's. I love my son and thank God for him. My overall family, though, was more scattered than ever. Again, the fault was mine. I still wasn't married; I was still far from forming my own family and fulfilling the dream of my childhood. I was still dating women at will. I was still out there.

The issue was patience. I didn't have much. I was twenty-five years old when I joined my third major league team, and I was impatient for something other than empire-building. I wasn't interested in looking down the road. I wanted to win immediately. I wanted a pennant and a World Series. And I wanted to be part of a team that would go down in history.

Marlins general manager Dave Dombrowski called me into his office. He was a serious guy.

"We're going to ask you for something, Gary," he said, "that no one has ever asked you for before."

"What's that?" I wanted to know.

"Patience."

"That's not my strength," I admitted.

"It's going to have to be," he said, "because it's the key to this team. You're the key to this team. We're building this team on your shoulders."

"That's a heavy statement," I said.

"It's a true statement, and a true reflection of our opinion of you. We see you as more than an All-Star. We see you as a leader, a guy with the guts and drive to get everyone going. Every team needs a motivator, and you're ours. You're our franchise."

"I don't know what to say."

"You don't have to say anything," said Dombrowski. "I realize this is new for you. The Brewers didn't treat you right. You did great with the Padres, but the Padres are in the process of throwing away their team. When we got you, we got lucky."

"When you say 'patient,' exactly *how* patient do you mean?" I asked.

"Five years," he answered.

"Five years is a long time."

"In five years, Gary, you're going to lead us to a World Series. I could blow smoke up your butt and tell you we'll do it in two or even three, but I want to be honest. I don't want to create false expectations. We see you as a lifetime Marlin. We see you coming home to the state where you were born, the place that you love and the place that loves you. You're going to be a big man here, Gary. You're going to be a leader."

I was flattered. Who wouldn't be? The icing on the cake was when I met the owner, Wayne Huizenga, who explained why he'd named the team the Marlins.

"I'm a deep-sea fisherman," said Huizenga, "and I fish for marlins. Marlins are the biggest challenge because they're fighters. They're strong and they're fierce. That's how we see you, Shef. You're a Marlin."

That kind of talk got to me. No owner had talked to me like that before. What they said boiled down to one thing: responsibility. I was being given responsibility not only for myself, but also for an entire team. That meant I had to be accountable.

I thought about my dad, the most responsible of men. I thought about my grandfather, a guy who'd always been accountable to his employer and family. Now I was being elevated to their level. I was growing up. I was being treated as a man.

A multiyear plan isn't easy for a twenty-five-year-old to embrace. But I was beginning to see its benefits. It wasn't a hyped-up goal. It wasn't frantic or crazy. If anything, it took off the pressure. And when Padre manager Greg Riddoch had taken the pressure off me, I'd responded by winning the batting crown. Maybe a no-pressure five-year plan could do the same thing.

What at first had seemed a drawback—a first-year expansion

team with no history—now seemed like an attraction. Because the team had no history, it had no baggage. I could help make its history. There were no ghosts, no curses; everything was sparkling new.

Then there was Miami. I'd never lived in Miami. Compared to Miami, Tampa was the sticks. The early eighties was still "Miami Vice" time. Miami was jumping, the coolest city in the country. Miami was all about fast cars, fast boats, and fast women. Miami was the place where successful young men wanted to live, and sexy young women wanted to be discovered.

I found myself in the center of all that. South Beach. Hip bars. Celebrity parties.

I'd come home to Florida, but to a Florida I'd never really known before.

RAGE

Rage will make you sick—maybe not physically sick, but spiritually sick.

In those years that I played for the Marlins, I played with rage.

Losing enraged me.

Striking out enraged me.

Getting a bad call enraged me.

Watching our team sink in the standings enraged me.

I was an angry man.

Yet, at the same time, I never left the ballpark with fewer than six fine women. I had a fancy car and a fancy house on the water. When it came to the pleasures of life, I had anything I wanted whenever I wanted it. That's how I rolled.

My rage had nothing to do with contracts or money. Huizenga

and I got along great. After I was traded to the Marlins in June of 1993, I made the All-Star Team and raised my slugging percentage. Despite serious pain in my right shoulder, I hung in and gave it my all.

"We believe in you, Gary," Dombrowski kept repeating.

Management put their money where their mouth was: In 1994, they gave me a four-year contract that was eventually extended six more years. The Marlins wound up giving me ten years in contracts and many millions in salary, with never a word of disagreement from me.

Then why the rage?

I didn't mind being moved from third base to right field. I kept hearing Grandpa saying, "A good player can play anywhere." I got the hang of the outfield in a hurry. I liked making circus catches and nailing runners. I got into hardcore fielding so fiercely that I messed up my left rotator cuff trying to make an impossible grab. That cost me weeks on the bench. But playing only eighty-seven games, I still wound up the year hitting twenty-seven homers and seventy-eight RBIs. My fielding percentage was .970.

Then why the rage?

I was the go-to guy. They said I was the franchise, but the franchise wasn't going anywhere. I'd been advised to be patient, and I was trying, but patience wasn't my style. Losing wasn't my style.

When the 1994 season ended in August because of the players' strike, the Marlins were in the cellar. Our record was 51–63.

On the outside, I was cool. I didn't lash out. You'd think I had it together. But I didn't like playing in Joe Robbie Stadium when the stands were half empty and there wasn't a chance in the world we'd get to the play-offs.

I thought about Doc in New York. I thought how Doc had played for the Mets during their championship run. I thought of the size of the crowds and the excitement of those games. It was like the fate of the world was riding on every pitch. I also thought of how so much had changed for my uncle. In 1994, he was still a young man. He was twenty-nine. That season his record was 3–4 and his ERA 6.31. His habit was still haunting him. Baseball suspended him for the entire 1995 season. He was the greatest pitcher of his generation, and he was struggling as never before.

Maybe Doc was feeling the same hole in his soul that I was feeling. Maybe he was trying to fill it up with drugs.

Maybe I was trying to fill it up with rage. And women.

But no amount of drugs or rage or females can do the trick.

Eventually you come down from your high; you come down from your anger. And you face yourself.

Was it that I didn't like what I saw? I was a decent-looking guy. I provided for my parents. I provided for my three kids.

Was it my failure to build a family that got me so down?

Was it the fact that I was on a last-place team?

These were questions I didn't want to face, so I avoided them. Rather than look for solutions, I looked for distractions. A beautiful lady was a distraction. She boosted my ego. She made me feel important. She let me know I was a winner. She kept me from facing myself because, no matter how beautiful she might be, I was looking for someone even more beautiful.

THE CALMNESS

For the longest time it made me uncomfortable. I stayed away from it. In my mind, I called it the Calmness.

When Terry Pendleton joined the Marlins in 1995, I saw it right away. He had the Calmness.

He didn't get rattled. He didn't blow up. He didn't seem to be running around in his head. He was centered. He projected peace.

And that made me nervous.

Of course I respected Terry because he'd been such a spark plug, first for the Cards and then for the Braves. In 1991, he won the MVP, taking the Braves out of the basement to first place and a pennant. That year he hit .319 during the regular season and .367 in the World Series as his team lost to the Twins in seven games. Terry was a great infielder; the guy won three Gold Gloves.

When Terry and I became teammates he was thirty-five and I was twenty-six. I knew he possessed something I lacked. I knew he possessed something I wanted. It was that Calmness.

But I also saw him sitting in the locker room reading a Bible, and the last thing in the world I wanted to hear about was the Bible.

So I left Terry alone. I avoided the Calmness.

Meanwhile, the Marlins were getting better. With Terry, Chuck Carr, and Andre Dawson, we were climbing out of the cellar. We had a solid catcher in Charles Johnson, and Jeff Conine was slugging homers and knocking in runs.

I figured it would be my year, but I figured wrong.

I can still see vividly what happened that day: I was rounding second, ready to take third, when the center fielder charged the ball and fielded it perfectly. I slammed on the breaks and slipped on the wet infield. My feet lost contact with the ground and I went down on my thumb. I felt something crack. I figured I'd continue playing anyway, but when my arm swelled up to my elbow, I knew it was serious. X-rays showed a broken thumb.

They said surgery would mean I'd be out all year. I didn't believe that. But I did have to warm the bench June, July, and August. That was rough. Injuries are always rough. You play hard because you have to. You play hard because you want to. You play hard because there's no other way to play—not if you want to be great. But when you play hard you risk injury. You take chances. You mess up your body and find yourself frustrated, sitting around, waiting for the healing.

Waiting for the healing was my big challenge.

And seeing Terry with that Calmness didn't make things any easier.

My frustration built.

The trainer, a great guy named Larry Starr, said, "Don't even think about picking up a bat," but at the end of August when we were in Atlanta I snuck into the batting cage and took a few swings. No pain.

"No go," said Starr. "They want you ready for next year."

"The surgery went so well," I said. "I know I'm ready."

"Next year you'll be ready."

Still determined, I went on a strict diet of wheat grass and carrot juice and kept taking batting practice. I finally got a doctor up in New York to convince the trainer I was good to go.

The team was nervous but I wasn't. They finally put me back in the lineup on September 1. We were playing Houston in the Astrodome. The Astrodome is cavernous, not the favorite ballpark of home run hitters.

When I stepped up to the plate as the lead-off hitter in the second inning, I realized it had been three months since I'd faced a real pitcher in a real game. Greg Swindell was on the mound. I went into my stance, gave the bat my usual wiggle and focused on Greg's delivery. I saw the fastball coming, high and inside. I nailed the sucker and sent it sailing some 460 feet. Trotting the bases, I knew my injury problems were behind me.

That September I hit nine more homers, twenty-seven RBIs, and wound up the season hitting .324.

"Your on base percentage was .467," said Dombrowski. "Next year you're going to demolish this league, Gary. I know you are."

Before I could do that, though, something happened that had me thinking even more about Terry Pendleton and his Calmness.

I got shot.

IT STARTED OUT
AS ONE OF THOSE
UNEVENTFUL
DAYS . . .

The season was over. Florida finished 22½ games behind the Braves, but we'd managed to move out of the cellar. I left Miami feeling halfway hopeful. Before I left the city, Terry said he wanted to talk to me, but I knew what that would be about.

"We'll talk during the off-season," I said, though my intention was to keep avoiding the guy.

Something, though, was drawing me to Terry's inner peace.

I drove my big white Mercedes back to Tampa. When I rode around the old neighborhood, which I did from time to time, I kept my .45 in the front seat, just for safety. In the old neighborhood, you never knew what to expect. But on this particular day, because I was picking up my daughter, I put the gun in the trunk.

I was due to see Carissa at 3 P.M., but I was a little early.

When I called from the car phone, she wasn't home yet. So I decided just to ride around until she got there.

I pulled up to the corner of Martin Luther King, Jr. and North Fortieth Street. Spotted a guy on foot approaching my car. I figured I knew him. Maybe an old friend. Maybe someone who recognized me and wanted an autograph. But being the kind of guy who keeps the windows rolled up and doors locked, I kept them locked until I saw who it was.

What I saw was a brother with a gun.

"Get out!" he barked.

I wasn't getting out.

He aimed the gun right at me and fired. He was less than an arm's length away from me when he pulled the trigger. The bullet penetrated the window and hit me in the chest. As I fell on the floor, I reached for my gun in the glove compartment, forgetting it was in the trunk. A shot from my .45 would have given the thug quite a surprise, but I didn't have my .45.

I looked over to my right side to see if he had an accomplice. He didn't.

The guy kept screaming, "Get out! Get out!"

But he wasn't getting my car. He wasn't getting anything.

Crouched down, my adrenaline racing, my heart hammering, I saw blood on my shirt but, for reasons I didn't understand, I didn't feel pain. By now cars were honking and the shooter was running.

I whipped the Benz around in a frantic U-turn, determined to run him down. But he was jumping fences and running through yards. I couldn't get to him. And my blood was flowing.

I had to think fast. I called my buddy who owned a barbershop down the block and told him I'd be in there in a second; I told him to call an ambulance and my folks so they wouldn't hear about the shooting from the news.

When I arrived at the barbershop, a crowd was waiting. They

put me in a barber's chair, gave me a cold towel. The wound was far from critical.

But the incident was.

The incident stopped me dead in my tracks.

Some of the papers played up the confrontation like I was involved with bad guys who were paying me back. Nothing could be further from the truth. Reporters speculated on all kinds of stuff.

The simple truth was that someone I didn't know from Adam had tried to carjack me.

Maybe he knew who I was; maybe he didn't. Probably he just saw a big Mercedes as a lucrative score.

I was hesitant to tell people what had happened because I didn't think they'd believe me: I'd been shot at point blank range. The bullet had penetrated the glass and miraculously stopped short of entering my body and piercing my heart.

How could I explain it?

I couldn't.

I healed up quickly, but my soul stayed in shock.

If Terry's Calmness had touched me before, I felt doubly touched now. Was someone or something trying to get my attention? If so, it worked.

I couldn't stop replaying the whole thing: How did I escape being murdered? *Why* did I escape? And now that I'd escaped, where was I supposed to put my gratitude? Who was I grateful to—luck, fate, or God?

I don't care who you are—when someone points a gun at you and shoots, your world is never the same—even if you survive with a minor injury. *Especially* if you survive.

You look for what it symbolizes. You look for the meaning. You look at your fears, your life; you remember what you've done right and what you've done wrong.

Given all this soul-searching, you'd think I might decide to see what Terry's Calmness was all about. Every night and every day I was feeling more and more moved by Terry's spirit. But I still wasn't ready.

Instead of lying low and making some healthy vows, I raised the stakes. I got a luxury penthouse in Miami overlooking Biscayne Bay. I hung out with celebrity friends. I found more gorgeous women. Because I'd done well in my career and because I'd escaped from the jaws of death, I reasoned that I was entitled.

Man, "entitled" is a powerful word. It'll take you to all sorts of places and put you in all sorts of situations.

My arrogance was strong:

Don't tell me what to do.

Don't tell me where to go.

I've got money.

I've got talent.

Don't get in my way.

MAN ON FIRE

n the first month of the 1996 season I hit eleven home runs. I was happy to get in a full season. In 161 games, I wound up with forty-two home runs, 120 RBIs, and a batting average of .314. I also drew 142 walks.

The Marlins did a little better—we finished two games under .500—but it was the Braves' year until they got beat by the Yankees in the World Series. That was the year the Yankees' new dynasty began its reign.

The 1996 Yankees are remembered for Derek Jeter, Mariano Rivera, Tino Martinez, Andy Pettitte, David Cone, and all the others. But my biggest memory of that team—a memory of a feat bigger than any of my own accomplishments—goes back to May 14. That was the day my uncle Dwight pitched a no-hitter.

The Yanks had signed Doc as a free agent that year. He was

especially thrilled because it meant once again being on the same team as Darryl Strawberry, his buddy when they were together on the Mets. He kept saying, "I got something to prove and I'm going to prove it."

That day we were pounding the Cardinals in Miami, but when word came from Yankee Stadium that Dwight had thrown a hitless game, tears came to my eyes. First I called Doc, then my mom. She was crying too. My thoughts turned to Grandpa. His health had been bad for many years. He'd been on kidney dialysis since 1986, and was now in the hospital waiting on open-heart surgery. I called to see if he'd been able to listen to the game on the radio. He had. "Smiling all the time," the nurse said. "Just nodding his head and smiling."

As the year went on, I felt myself becoming The Man. When you're crushing home runs and terrorizing pitchers, it's hard not to feel powerful. Hard not to feel invulnerable.

Everything Huizenga had said was coming true. I *was* the franchise. The Marlins *were* getting better. My skills as a hitter and fielder *were* turning me into one of baseball's premier players.

I was on top of the world.

Or was I?

And if wasn't, what was wrong?

Inside—deep, deep down—I didn't feel like The Man. I felt empty. I'd sit in my big apartment overlooking the bay and stare into space. Didn't know what to do or what to think. I'd study the sky. I'd study the water. I'd listen to a little music. I'd think about calling a woman. She'd chase the blues away. She'd take my mind off the loneliness. She'd fix me.

But how many times do you need to get fixed before you realize that the fix is fleeting?

A beautiful woman is a beautiful woman. She pleases your eyes. She satisfies your flesh. But you don't know her, and she doesn't know you. You don't connect to her soul. And your soul is still starving.

Flash and cash go only so far. Big plays and game-winning hits go only so far.

I was happy, but I was unhappy. I had everything I wanted, and I had nothing I wanted. I'd achieved it all, and I'd missed it all.

"Hey, Gary," Terry Pendleton said to me. "You seem restless, man."

Terry knew. Terry always knew. But Terry had the Calmness, and the Calmness was still scaring me off. Terry had that Bible, and that Bible was something I didn't need.

"I'm okay, Terry," I said.

"You're better than okay," he said. "Man, you're blessed. It's a blessing for me to have you in my life."

Why did he have to talk that way? Why was he always so positive, so understanding, so downright loving? Why couldn't he just leave me alone?

"Tim Cash is in town," Terry said. "I'm going to meet him over at Denny's for lunch. Why don't you join us?"

I knew that Tim Cash, who'd been signed by the Astros in the 1980s, was a Christian who ministered to other baseball players. I knew what he and Terry wanted. I knew I needed to avoid them.

"Don't worry, Gary," said Terry, reading my mind. "We're not going to make you sign on the dotted line."

I agreed.

What harm could it do?

I'd listen to their pitch, I'd eat a cheeseburger, I'd leave.

As soon as I met Tim, I saw he had it. The Calmness. That made me even more nervous. Two Calmness guys versus me.

We sat in a booth and ordered lunch. The talk was all about baseball. Not a word about God. Tim was like Terry—open, friendly, the kind of guy who didn't have to talk about himself all the time. He asked me lots of questions, but nothing too personal.

I was waiting for the big conversion push, but the pitch never came. Terry and Tim were just being friendly to a guy in obvious pain. And I suppose it was their acceptance of me that got me to open up.

"I don't feel all that good inside," I said. "Haven't felt good for a long time."

"What do you think it is?" asked Tim.

"I got a lot of stuff," I said. "Maybe getting out from under all that stuff isn't easy."

"Sure isn't," Terry agreed. "The world's always pulling us back."

"Just as God's always pulling us to Him," said Tim. "That's the beautiful part. He never stops pulling."

"I been feeling that pull," I confessed. "Been feeling it strong."

"Tell Tim about the shooting, Gary," Terry urged.

I told him.

"Amazing," said Tim. "The bullet breaks your skin but never goes any further. What do you make of that?"

"I have to call it a miracle."

"Do you feel like you're called to tell the story?" asked Terry.

"I'd tell it, but who'd believe me?" I asked.

"You'll know when to tell it," said Terry. "And you'll know how to tell it. The thing is this, man. We all think we're living our own story. We think we're the producer, the director, and the star of our own story. We get self-obsessed. That's human nature, especially when you achieve prominence. But that role of producer/director/star is enough pressure to do us in. Meanwhile, we're missing the big story. God is the big story. When we see that, when we realize we're part of His story, we can finally relax. Because in His story we're accepted and loved in a way that the world will never accept or love us. In His story we don't have to worry about winning. In His story we've already won."

"That's the Calmness," I said.

"Is that what you call it?" asked Terry.

"You got the Calmness," I repeated.

"I got God. And so do you—only you don't know it."

I left that lunch touched by everything that had been said. I was touched by their concern and I was touched that they brought out feelings in me I hadn't expressed to anyone. I admitted that I was caught up in a whirlwind of women. I talked about the hole in my soul. I said how, even in the middle of a great year, an emptiness haunted me.

I admitted—and this was the biggest admission of all—that I needed God.

We prayed before we left.

"Father God," said Terry, "we just want to thank You for this fellowship and the fact that men can gather in Your name and openly and honestly say how we feel. We pray for Gary, that he might find peace and meaning in his life. We pray that he turns to You for comfort, for strength, for loving salvation. In Jesus' precious name, Amen."

I could hardly sleep that night. Tossing and turning, I thought—what do I need with Jesus? Do I really need salvation? Didn't I save myself by learning to hit a baseball? Don't I meet my own needs by providing for my family and myself? Wasn't I my own savior? Aren't we all our own saviors?

In spite of my questions, though, I prayed silently. Prayed for direction. Prayed for peace of mind. Prayed for clarity and understanding. Prayed myself to sleep.

When I awoke in the morning, I realized that my spiritual journey had begun.

I hate to tell you where that journey began, but the truth is the truth.

It began by my trying to make deals with God.

DEAL NUMBER 1

L ord, let me win a World Series and I'll serve You the rest of
my days.

I know it sounds childish, but I'd read that Jesus said,
"Come to me as a child," and that's what I was doing.

You give me this, Lord, and I'll give you that.

Looking back, I see how I misunderstood the nature of God.
I see how I still wasn't ready to accept the Calmness. I was still
worked up, looking at the angles, trying to cut a deal.

I don't judge myself for that. It was where I was. Spiritual
journeys are just that—journeys. You have to begin somewhere.

I began reading the Bible and occasionally attending church.
I followed the sermons carefully. I was hungry for information
and I was hungry for truth. But I was also hungry for a World

Series victory. If God could help, why not? Why not do a little negotiation with the Almighty?

After all, the Marlins were negotiating for better players before the 1997 season. That's how they figured we could get competitive. That's how baseball works, and baseball was my reference point. It made sense to cut a deal with God.

Meanwhile, the Mariners cut lots of deals.

We got Moises Alou from Montreal and Bobby Bonilla from Baltimore. We also got Alex Fernandez from the White Sox who, together with Kevin Brown, Al Leiter, Livan Hernandez, and Robb Nen, formed a powerful pitching staff. Luis Castillo and Edgar Renteria were shaping up as a great double-play team. With a great new manager—Jim Leyland—I liked our chances.

In the last third of the 1996 season, Terry Pendleton was traded to the Braves, and in 1997 he played for the Reds, but we kept in touch.

"Do you feel like a pawn when the owners trade you here and then trade you there?" I asked him.

"Yeah, sometimes it bothers me," he said, "but that's just the business of the world. I don't take it that seriously. I know God's never going to trade me. I know that His love is constant. It goes on forever. He's my life, not some rich guy who owns a baseball team."

When Terry talked, I listened. He was different from any mentor I'd ever had. He wasn't a macho man. Macho meant nothing to him. He was a gentle man. He said that he wanted others to see the Jesus in him. From everything I read, Jesus was a gentle man. He got mad a couple of times, but that was rare. His way was to treat people gently; to show them love and under-standing; to meet them where they were.

Where was I?

I was in mourning.

On January 10, 1997, Dan Edward Gooden died.

At the funeral, I stood by my parents, my cousin Derek, Dwight, my aunts, and my grandmother.

My mind was flooded with memories.

This was the man who'd gotten me started, who'd taught me the game, who'd given me attitude and determination. Without Grandpa, I'd have no career. He pushed me. He promised me that hard work would pay off. He led the way.

He also taught me. He kept harping on that Inside Power. "Nothing can replace it," he said. "Nothing can stop it."

Thinking about that Inside Power and Terry's Calmness, I wondered if the two were related. If you had Inside Power, you'd have the Calmness. And vice versa.

Death is a sobering thing. You see someone who's been with you every step of the way—every crisis, every celebration—lowered into the ground. You say good-bye, but you can't believe he's gone.

"He's not," said Terry, when I called him the next day. "His spirit is with God, and God is in you. Your grandfather will be with you forever."

My grief went on, but so did life. A new season was starting.

I began it optimistically. I always do. I expected my best year ever.

It didn't happen. April through August, my numbers were mediocre.

The press got on me, but the press got on everyone. They got on the Marlins for trying to "buy a championship" with off-season trades. If the team hadn't made deals, the press would have accused management of doing nothing to improve our chances. You can't win with the press.

Before the season, Huizenga gave me a six-year $61 million contract. The negotiations went great, with no arguments from me. In fact, I'd never gotten into a negotiations wrangle. That wasn't my style. I'd had a strong 1996 and was being rewarded. So when I started out 1997 slowly, the writers started beating up on me, saying I didn't deserve the reward. Naturally, part of me wanted to beat up on them—with my fists. But another part was listening to Terry Pendleton, whose laid-back approach was "Everyone's got a job to do. The press's job is to be negative, because negative sells. Our job is to hit home runs because home runs bring fans to the ballpark. But the biggest job of all is to remember that the victory is already ours. Our victory is in Christ—and that's nothing anyone or anything can change."

Victory in Christ was fine, but I still wanted victory on the diamond. I still wanted to show the reporters—and the fans— that I was worth the big money I was getting.

That was a mistake. On the baseball field especially, it's always a mistake to try to prove something to someone. That kind of motivation seems good, but it really interferes with the naturalness of your game. You're too anxious; you swing too early; you swing too late; you try too hard. You gotta forget expectations and get back into the zone. Just be where you are, not where you hope to be.

Well, that kind of thinking is wise, but I couldn't get there. I was thinking of showing everyone I was worth the money. And that kept me struggling. Meanwhile, though, the Marlins were having the best season in our history. This was the year that Dombrowski had said we'd win the championship. His trades were working. Jim Leyland's strategy was working. Leyland knew I wasn't about to make excuses for myself, but he also knew I was hampered by a super-sore hamstring. All he said to me—and to the reporters bashing me—was, "Shef will be there when we need him."

We didn't win our division. The Braves won with a 101–61 record, but our ninety-one victories secured us a wild-card berth.

The first round of the play-offs pitted Atlanta against Houston and us against the Giants. The Giants meant Barry Bonds.

Bonds had his usual great year—forty homers, 101 RBIs, 145 walks. Everyone considered Barry one of the premier players. I'd been put in that category as well, but this year my doubters had reason to question whether I deserved that ranking.

I respected Barry and he respected me. We saw ourselves as hard workers and tough trainers. But of course, like all athletes, we were also intense competitors. To face him in a play-off situation got my juices flowing. My attitude was *Whatever Bonds does, I have to do more.*

So many emotions were running through me. I wanted to turn around a so-so year and end with a spectacular post-season performance. I wanted not to worry about being spectacular so I could chill out and just hit the ball. I wanted to test God and see if He was really serious about getting me a World Series ring.

I wanted to win.

Game 1. October 1. Joe Robbie Stadium, Miami. Hot day. Hot game. The Giants hadn't been in the play-offs since 1989—so they were hungry. The Marlins hadn't been in the play-offs ever—so we were hungry.

Intense pitching battle, Kevin Brown for us, Kirk Rueter for them. Bonds doubled in the seventh. I doubled in the eighth. Coming up in the bottom of the ninth, we were locked in a 1–1 tie. With the bases loaded, Edgar Renteria singled to right, driving in our winning run.

Game 2. We were still in Florida, and I was feeling good because in game 1, I'd gotten on base three out of four times.

This time the game was even more thrilling. Bonds went two for four. I went three for four.

In the bottom of the sixth, I smacked a towering upper-deck home run.

Going into the top of the ninth, we were up 6–5. The Giants tied the score at 6–6.

Bottom of the ninth: I singled to left, then stole second. Bonilla walked. Then Moises Alou blooped a single into shallow center-field. I took off, determined to score the winning run. Wasn't sure I could beat the throw, but I was hustling like crazy. Centerfielder had a clean shot at the plate. He might have nailed me, but his throw hit the pitcher's mound, flew up in the air, and I slid home safe.

Marlins 2, Giants zip.

Game 3. San Francisco.

It was do or die for the Giants. They died. The crushing blow came in the sixth: Devon White's monster grand slam put us up 4–2. We eventually won 6–2.

We swept San Francisco.

Next up, Atlanta.

The Braves represented a different challenge. Atlanta was deep into their dynasty. They won 101 games in 1997; they were the team of Tom Glavine and Greg Maddux, John Smoltz and Jeff Blauser, Chipper and Andruw Jones, Kenny Lofton and my friend Fred McGriff. They were tough and the odds were with them.

"Are you with me, God?" I asked. "Is our deal still good? I get the World Series and you get me."

We'd soon see.

In the series against the Giants, I'd hit .556. If I could keep it up against the Braves, I'd feel like the light of the Lord was definitely shining on me.

Well, the series wasn't close. We pounded Atlanta 4 games to 2, and I got on base eleven of twenty-four times.

Next stop, World Series.

God was looking good.

No expansion team had ever made it to the World Series this quickly. The press kept saying Huizenga had bought the pennant, but there were other owners trying to do the same thing. We got there because we earned it.

The Indians got there by beating the Yankees and the Orioles. They had a good year, with strong pitching from Charles Nagy and Orel Hershiser and strong hitting from Dave Justice, Sandy Alomar, Manny Ramirez, Omar Vizquel, and Tony Fernandez.

It was shaping up to be a great series.

My adrenaline was pumping. The only other World Series I'd been to was eleven years before, when the Mets had beaten Boston. I'd gone to watch Doc. Now Doc was watching me. Amazing.

The dream of a lifetime.

Dombrowski's dream.

Huizenga's dream.

My dream.

The first World Series game in my state.

The first game has sixty-seven thousand screaming fans crowded into our ballpark.

The first game we clobber Hershiser and win, 7–4. Bonilla goes two for three, Moises Alou and Charles Johnson hit back-to-back home runs.

Second game: The Indians clobber Kevin Brown and win, 6–1.

Series moves to Cleveland.

Cleveland feels like Alaska. Wind-chill factor in the twenties. Everyone says the boys from Florida, spoiled by the sun, will freeze.

Instead we explode. And so do the Indians. No matter how much offense we put up, they match it. It's a dogfight.

I homer in the first, walk in the third, double in the seventh.

Going into the top of the ninth, we're deadlocked 7–7.

After three Indian errors, three walks, and a wild pitch, we've put up seven more runs and lead 14–7 going into the bottom of the ninth. The Tribe comes back with four runs, but that's not enough. Marlins 14, Indians 11.

I wind up with three hits and five RBIs.

We're up 2 games to 1.

Snowfall in Cleveland. Manny Ramirez and Matt Williams don't mind; they each crush two-run homers and the Indians win in a walk, 10–3.

Series tied.

Last series game in Cleveland

Hershiser back on the mound. Hershiser gets shelled again. But this time the game's a thriller.

We score two in the second inning, they score one. But then in the third Sandy Alomar smashes a huge three-run homer.

In the top of the sixth, I single, Bonilla walks, and Alou connects for a three-run blast off Hershiser—his third homer of the series—and we're back in the game. A bases loaded walk gives us a 6–4 lead.

Top of the eighth, Alou scores another run and we're up by three.

Bottom of the eighth. Matt Williams leads off with a single to center. Jim Thome at bat. Thome tripled earlier in the game. He's a powerhouse who hit forty home runs during the season. I play him deep, but not quite deep enough. He lifts one to right field. It looks like it's going over my head into the seats. It looks like it's gone. I chase it with everything in me. I go back, back, back. All I can see is the ball. I can't see the fans, can't see the stands, can't see the wall. Just the ball.

I leap higher than I've ever leaped before.

And bring it down safely in my glove.

Center fielder Devon White, normally unemotional, lets his emotions go wild. He's screaming. My whole team turns to acknowledge me.

Later, friends watching the game on TV tell me that Bob Costas called it "the play of the series."

The play turns everything around.

Now the momentum is with us.

Alou singles in a run in the ninth, putting us up 8–4.

But Cleveland won't go away. In the bottom of the ninth, they get close; they roar back with three runs. But Robb Nen gets Alomar to fly out for the final run and we win the thing, 8–7.

Now it's back to Miami with the Marlins up, 3 games to 2.

One more victory and we're World Champs.

Game 6 sets up Game 7. Game 6 is all about Chad Ogea's fine pitching and shortstop Omar Vizquel robbing Charles Johnson of a sure hit that would have driven in two runs for us in the sixth inning.

Tribe 4, Marlins 1.

I go zero for three.

It all comes down to one game.

Before the game, I pray. I remind God, as if it were my job to remind the Lord, that we have a deal.

Honor it and you've got me. Dishonor it and I'm gone.

Looking back, it's amazing to me that I was actually threatening God. My spirit had a lot to learn, but my mind was fixated on winning a championship ring.

It's our Al Lieter versus their Jaret Wright.

They draw first blood and score two in the third.

We're shut out until the bottom of the seventh, when Bobby Bonilla hits a monster home run.

Indians 2, Marlins 1.

We don't score in the eighth.

When we go to bat in the bottom of the ninth, we're up against it.

Everyone knows Cleveland is the favorite. They haven't won the Series since 1948. They're overdue. We're the new kids on the block. We've done well to come this far, but this is the end of the road.

Three outs and they have us.

Alou singles, and hope is alive.

But Bonilla strikes out.

Then Charles Johnson singles to right and Moises takes third.

Craig Counsell at bat. Craig's had a good year. Craig's steady. Craig can do it. Craig gets good wood on a fastball and drives it to right. The ball is caught but Alou scores.

Tie, 2–2.

We're going into extra innings.

An extra inning in a seventh game can give a healthy man a heart attack.

An extra inning in a seventh game is a thrill to watch, but to play in a game like that is otherworldly. The intensity level is like nothing I've ever experienced before.

Top of the tenth, Cleveland can't score.

Bottom of the tenth, our chance to go home with all the marbles.

Renteria singles.

I single.

Two on, one out.

One hit and it's over.

But Cangelosi is called on strikes, and Alou flies to right.

Take a deep breath; we're going into the eleventh with our lives on the line.

A double play ends a small Cleveland threat.

We go up in the bottom of the eleventh, still tied 2–2.

Bonilla opens up with a single.

We're all standing at the edge of the dugout.

Zaun bunts out, can't get Bonilla in scoring position.

But Counsell reaches first on an error.

Men on first and second, one out.

Devon White hits a grounder to second, but Bonilla is nailed at the plate.

Runners on second and third, two out.

Edgar Renteria at bat.

I'm in the on-deck circle.

I'm watching like a hawk.

I see the pitch coming in.

I see what Renteria sees.

I see his arms move, his wrists turn, his bat meeting the ball.

His bat kissing the ball right on the mouth.

The ball shooting up the middle of the infield.

Looks like Tony Fernandez, a fine fielder, will nab it, but . . .

He doesn't!

Ball goes up on Tony's glove!

The ball's in center field!

A hit!

A run!

A World Series!

We're jumping and screaming and yelling, and all I'm thinking is, *God is real! God is real! God is real! God is real!*

DEAL NUMBER 2

Deal number 1 was ridiculous. All deals with God are ridiculous. God is love. God can't be anything *but* love. That's His nature. He loves the World Series losers as much as the winners, the poor and the rich, the homeless and the guy who lives in a mansion. God isn't in the business of cutting deals with guys like me who are looking for material gain. At least not the God I worship now.

But back then, I was still stumbling along the spiritual path. I didn't know it, but I was still confused about the nature of God. And I was still a hypocrite. The proof is what happened after we won the Series.

I did fall on my knees and thank God.

But then, to be honest, I forgot about God. I forgot about our deal. I forgot that I'd promised him my heart in exchange for this victory.

I got distracted. The locker-room celebration distracted me. All the shouting distracted me. All the memories of Dombrowski and Huizenga saying we'd do this distracted me. And the champagne. And the cigars. And the reporters. And the slaps on the back and the words of praise.

Doc was there.

"My dad would be so proud," he said. "I'm proud."

"Thanks, Doc," I said. "Let's go down to South Beach and party some more."

"Aren't you tired, Bug?"

"Not really, man, I'm pumped."

"Well, I'm drained, I'm going home."

Strange, but I couldn't get anyone to go to South Beach to party. Strange, too, that I was ready to party rather than, as promised, turn my life over to God.

And the strangest part of all was that South Beach, party capital of the world, was partied out. Hardly anyone was there. The place looked deserted. I couldn't understand why, but as I drove around in the back of a long limo, I didn't see anything happening.

After this amazing victory, I suddenly felt a pang of loneliness. Deep loneliness.

I found other parties. They roped off the street in St. Petersburg where my family all had houses and strung a sign that said, "Welcome Home, Gary, World Champ." I rolled up to that block party with a friend and five women. We partied all night. We partied the next week in L.A., where I went on Jay Leno's show. The parties went on for weeks.

From time to time, I thanked God, but the parties were taking up more of my time than the prayers. The parties left me empty. What should have been the happiest time in my life was becoming the loneliest. The birth of my second son, Garrett, filled me with joy. All my children are precious blessings. Garrett's mom was a woman I knew in Miami. But because she and I weren't destined for a long-term relationship, my loneliness only deepened.

In terms of baseball, God had answered my prayer. Before it happened, I had thought a World Series ring would fill the hole in my soul. I had the ring, but the hole was still there. If anything, the hole had gotten deeper.

I kept moving, flying from city to city, thinking another celebration, another spot on a talk show, another interview about our tremendous victory would make me feel better. Those things were fun, but once they were over, they were over. Then I had to face myself.

This went on for months. Then in February I was invited to the NBA All-Star game in New York. I figured that'd be fun— more parties, more distraction. I got to the city, checked into the Hilton hotel where all the action was happening, and went up to my room to shower and change.

In that short period of time, a powerful emotion hit me. It was like the feeling I felt when I first met Terry Pendleton, but it was also different. It said, *You're alone, you have no commitment, you have no woman, you have no wife.*

I fell on my knees and prayed. "*God, I need a righteous woman, a strong woman to anchor my household, to anchor me just as I can anchor her. This loneliness, Lord, is killing me. This feeling of having everything and having nothing is making me crazy, Lord. Deal two won't be like Deal one. You don't have any reason to trust me, Lord, except you can look inside my heart and see I'm sincere. I've read Proverbs 18: 'He who finds a wife finds a good thing.' I want that good thing. I'll know her when I see her, Lord, and I praise You for sending her to me."*

Ten minutes later, I took the elevator to the lobby and, right there in the middle of all the noise and the action—among the athletes, reporters, stars, fans, agents, PR execs, bartenders, waitresses, among the men looking for women and women looking for men—I heard her voice. In the faint light I saw her face. I was immediately drawn to her.

A friend of mine knew a friend of hers. They introduced us.

"I'm DeLeon," she said.

"I'm Gary."

We were standing.

"We can sit over there and talk," I said. "It'll be quieter."

I led us to a corner table. I felt her hesitancy.

"It's okay to sit down," I urged. "I don't bite."

We sat.

"You been to a lot of these things?" I asked.

"No," she said. "This is my first." Her voice was so soft I had to lean in to hear. She projected a sweetness I'd never felt in a woman before. Her sweetness was so powerful I felt unguarded. She was thin and energetic—dark hair, bright dark eyes, and a smile that lit up my soul.

"How about you?" she asked. "Do you come to these events frequently?"

"Well, sometimes. It's part of my job."

She didn't ask about my job. I could tell she didn't know who I was. As it turned out, I didn't know who she was. We were both professionals, famous in our fields, but neither of us had a clue. We were just happy talking to each other.

"To be honest," I said, "I told myself not to go to these kinds of crazy weekends, but here I am, right in the middle of one."

"Why did you tell yourself that?" asked DeLeon.

"They make me lonely."

"I understand."

"You do?" I said.

"Sure, room filled with people but no one really to talk to. And when we do talk, it's all on the surface. It's not exactly an easy place to spill your heart out."

"Is that what you're feeling from me?" I asked her. "You're feeling like I need to spill my heart out?"

"Maybe," she said.

"And you're willing to listen?"

"If it helps you."

"So you're saying I need help."

"We all do. Just like we all need God."

"So you're a Christian, DeLeon."

"I am."

"Figures."

"Why do you say that?" she asked.

"Your vibe."

"Thanks."

"I think I'm a Christian," I said.

"You *think* . . ."

"Well, I feel like I'm halfway there. I keep making deals with God."

"And how's that working out for you, Gary?"

"God keeps coming through on the deals, but I don't. And when I don't, well . . . I guess I pay the price."

"How?" she asked.

"I don't feel right. I feel lonely."

"Why do you think that is?"

"I think it has to do with how I messed up my family," I confessed. "When I started out in high school, I had this dream to have one wife and a bunch of kids under one roof."

"And now?"

"Now I have four kids under three different roofs and no wife."

"You feel like a family man without a family."

"Something like that. How about your family?"

"Well, there's my mom and dad."

"No sisters or brothers, no boyfriend, no kids."

"No," she said. "Mom and Dad are both preachers."

"That's deep."

"For the most part, that's been a blessing. And sometimes it's been a struggle."

"How do you mean?" I asked.

"Preachers' kids can be rebellious."

"And that was you—a rebel?"

"For a minute or two," she said, "I suppose so."

In very general terms, DeLeon spoke of her childhood. In very general terms, I spoke of mine.

I loved listening to her. Her voice was musical, gentle and relaxed. She didn't seem to have a judgmental bone in her body. She always got God into her stories. She spoke of how He led her. She spoke of God, not like someone she'd read about in books, but like someone she knew. A friend. A father. A protector. A faithful confidant.

Within fifteen minutes, she'd become my confidant. This had never happened to me before. I went into detail about the story of my daughters and the circumstances of their births. I talked about my sons. I described my disappointments in my life and in myself.

DeLeon just sat there and listened, nodding, understanding, asking me good questions that made me think. We spoke for almost an hour. When she got up to leave, I said, "Where you going?"

"I see my friend."

"Well, there's one thing I want to tell you before you go, DeLeon."

"What's that?"

"I'm going to marry you. You're going to be my wife."

Her reaction was quick. "You're crazy," she said. "You're *really* crazy."

And with that, she was gone.

Later that day, up in my room, I told my friend about DeLeon. I said that I thought I'd found the woman of my dreams.

"Well, think again, bro," he said, "cause I saw her in the lobby vibing with another man. They were deep into it."

"I don't believe it."

"Believe what you want to, but I'd leave this lady alone if I were you."

He wasn't me and I wasn't about to leave her alone.

When it was time to go out again, I passed through the lobby and there she was. Alone.

"So we run into each other for a second time," I said. "What do you think it means?"

"You tell me."

"I already told you. But you haven't even told me why you're here this weekend."

"My girlfriend's a writer. She's covering the game. She asked me to come along and keep her company."

"Well, I'd like you to keep me company. Tomorrow night Wyclef Jean is playing at this party. Can we go together?"

"I'll have to see," she said.

"See about what?"

"You're pushing this awfully hard."

"I can't let you go," I said.

"You're going to have to," she replied, "cause I'm on my way out."

My friend kept saying negative things. "Dog," he said, "there are so many fine young things running around here, why you chasing that one?"

Meanwhile, I wasn't chasing. I was praying.

I was praying that DeLeon would feel the connection.

I liked that she wasn't throwing herself at me. I liked that she was in her senior year in college. But I didn't like that she lived in Chicago. And I also didn't like that her tasteful and modest way of dressing didn't show me as much as I wanted to see.

When she agreed to go the Wyclef Jean party the next night, I hoped she'd wear something revealing. She didn't. She looked stunning, but covered up. Everything was subdued. My curiosity was on overdrive. She had perfect manners. She had great patience with all my stories. And the fact that she didn't drink or touch drugs made her that much more appealing. It was a great night that ended when I escorted her to her room. I was a gentleman . . .

Until I got back to my room and couldn't fall asleep. I kept thinking, *She's in her room, I'm in mine. Why can't we be in the same room?*

So I called her.

"It's Gary," I said.

"It's four A.M.," she said.

"Just want to see how you're doing."

"No, you don't," she said. "This is a booty call."

"Well . . ."

"Well, nothing," she said. "I don't like being woken up in the middle of the night and I don't respond to booty calls."

With that, she hung up in my ear.

Next morning she was leaving.

I came down to the lobby to see her off and apologize.

"I really am sorry," I said.

"I accept your apology."

"Can I have your cell number?"

"You can have my pager number."

"I have a policy of never taking a woman's pager number, only the cell."

"If you want to page me, Gary, that's fine. If you don't, I understand."

"I just want to make sure you get home safely."

I paged her that night. She responded.

"You get in all right?" I asked.

"Yes. It's nice of you to call."

"Can we keep talking?"

"Seems like that's what we're doing," she said.

The long-distance relationship heated up, at least from my point of view. As winter turned to spring, I called her all the time. I learned more about her. I learned that she was completing her degree at Lake Forest College, where she was a communications major. In September she would turn twenty-two. But for a young woman, she was amazingly accomplished. When she was fourteen, she'd appeared with Oprah Winfrey as an actress in the *Brewster Place* TV series. Long before that, though, as a six-year-old, she'd been a vocalist performing at a Chicago gospel festival with Andrae Crouch and James Cleveland. She learned organ and piano and released her first album when she was eight. The record was nominated for a Grammy, making her the youngest Grammy nominee ever. As a teenager, she kept making gospel records and gained a national reputation. Now, in addition to completing her education, she was interning at Harpo Productions, Oprah's company. I'd never known a lady like this before. She had her own agenda, her own ambition, her own

talent. She was independent and, to be honest, not all that interested in a man like me.

Whatever my defects, though, I was determined. I was in
love. I couldn't lose her. My old tactics weren't going to work.
Those tactics had gotten me lots of ladies, but never love. I knew
I couldn't afford to miss out this time. So I relied on the one quality that had served me since I was a kid: tenacity. I hung in there.

I'd hung in there when, as a little boy, Doc burned my hands
with his fastball. Hung in when I was kicked off the Little League
team. Hung in when I played under negative circumstances in
Milwaukee. Hung in when the Padres, a team I loved, traded me
to Florida. Hung in with the Marlins for five years until we were
able to turn it around. Hung in with several serious injuries.

I figured if I could hang in and meet my professional challenges, I could meet this challenge as well.

Except this time it wasn't a matter of being tough. It was a
matter of being persistent.

"I'm opening up my heart to you," I told DeLeon. "I've never
really done that before."

"I think that's beautiful," she replied. "I think that's wonderful."

But that wasn't the answer I wanted; I wanted her to say,
"Gary, I'm opening up my heart to you, too."

Weeks later, when I finally told her what I did for a living, she
didn't sound particularly impressed. All she said was that she
didn't follow baseball. On one hand, I hated hearing that because
I couldn't dazzle her with my achievements; but on the other
hand, if she ever came to like me, it would be because of who I
am, not what I do.

Slowly I felt her coming to like me. At least a little. When
spring training started in March, I invited her to Florida.

"If I do come," she said, "I'd want to bring someone with me."

"Anyone," I said. "Anyone you say."

"I'd want to bring my mother."

"That's fantastic."

"You like the idea?" she asked, sounding surprised.

"Why wouldn't I? You're the woman I want to marry. Naturally I want to get to know my future mother-in-law. You couldn't have made a better choice."

When they came down, it was a little awkward. They wanted to stay in a hotel. I'd just rented a big house with three bedrooms. I urged them to stay with me. We each had our own bedroom—me, DeLeon, and DeLeon's mom. By then I understood the rules.

Patience, patience, patience.

It was a little easier for me to find patience. I was feeling more of that Calmness that Terry had shown me. God's hand was surely in this. All I had to do was take my time and let the Lord lead.

The three of us spent time together. DeLeon's mom was great, as gracious and intelligent as her daughter. DeLeon and I were rarely alone, and when we were it was only for short drives in the car.

That's when we began talking more about the deals I'd been making with God. This time she was more direct with me.

"It's not about you, Gary, it's about Him."

"But it's my life."

"No," she corrected me. "It's about Him living His life through you. When you go to God, you don't go as a negotiator. You go to Him as a child. You go to Him admitting all your fears and faults."

I'd just sit and listen. I wouldn't argue. I didn't have the background or knowledge to argue with DeLeon about faith. I might have been eight years older than her, but she was raised up in a righteous church.

"I don't want you to think I'm perfect," she said, "because I'm not. I've had my challenges. I did things I'm not proud of. But I always came back to Him. I don't want to sound pious,

Gary, but I learned that I can't live without Him. I really can't."

"And I can't live without you," I said.

I waited for her response, but instead she stayed silent.

The season started and I stayed on course. I had two goals—winning DeLeon's heart and winning another World Series for Florida.

Then something happened that turned me around and changed everything.

It came from out of the blue.

FIRE SALE!

Grandpa was gone but his wisdom haunted me. I kept hearing him say, "Baseball can break your heart."

I didn't think it would happen again, not in the aftermath of our historic World Series win. We were the darlings of the state. We were heroes. I'd stuck it out with the team for five years—five years of building, five years of hard work and pure desire. Now we were there. With our talent, the 1998 Marlins figured to be contenders. A new dynasty was under way.

But by May, only a month into the new season, the dynasty was dead.

What had happened?

Owner Wayne Huizenga didn't get what he wanted. He wanted the city to fund a new stadium. He'd been unsuccessfully trying for years. When we won the Series, he was sure it would happen. He felt entitled. He'd spent a fortune on salaries. He'd put together the perfect rainbow coalition team with a great mix of nationalities. He'd made everyone happy. His team was filled with All-Stars.

So when Huizenga was told again that the city wasn't building a stadium for him, he flipped. In essence he said, "The hell with you." And just like that, he dumped the team that had pulled off the miraculous win. Within a span of a few months, he managed to get rid of Moises Alou, Robb Nen, Kevin Brown, Devon White, and Jeff Conine. The big blow, though, happened in mid-May, when he proposed trading me, Bobby Bonilla, Charles Johnson, Jim Eisenreich and Manuel Barrios to the Dodgers for Mike Piazza and Todd Zeile.

The idea of the trade broke my heart—for many reasons.

First, I'd just begun to believe again in a team, a family, a fellowship of winners. I'd bought into the notion of this five-year plan ending in not just a single victory, but years of victories to come. The Marlins would take their place as a powerhouse team along with the Braves, the Yankees, and the Dodgers. I'd see that, despite my early disillusionments, baseball was about more than business. Baseball was about a dream coming true. But now, once again, the dream had turned bad.

Second, I was home and wanted to stay home. My family was here. My life was here. I had no interest in moving to L.A.

Third, if I were traded to the Dodgers, I wanted to play *with* Mike Piazza, not against him. Piazza was great, just the kind of player I wanted on my team. The Dodgers minus Mike weren't all that interesting to me.

Last, and most painful of all, was the feeling of betrayal. Huizenga had been like a dad to me. But the way he was dismantling the franchise—the same franchise he'd promised would be built around me—hurt my heart. I was being deserted. I understood that he was a businessman and business is about money.

But I also knew that, if he'd wanted to, he could have found a way to keep this team together. Instead he threw us in the Dumpster like stale garbage.

But the irony was this:

I didn't *have* to go. I was holding the ace. I'd signed a six-year blanket no-trade clause with the Marlins. I could kill the trade by staying where I was.

The dilemma, though, was that staying would mean going down with a losing team. The Marlins were doomed to sink to last place—which they did. Did I want to settle for a losing team when the Dodgers were perennial winners?

Even more pressing were the attitudes of my teammates who were part of the trade. They wanted to go to California; I was the only one holding them back.

Bonilla came up to me and said, "Hey, Gary, I'm dreaming of driving my Porsche through the Hollywood Hills."

Jim Eisenreich, a soft-spoken man whom I respected more than anyone, quietly said, "I know the position you're in, Gary, but I sure would like to make that move to L.A."

Charles Johnson pulled me aside. "My agent says the Dodgers will give me a five-year deal, so it'd be great if you could agree to this thing, Gary."

I was in a bind. I called DeLeon.

"What does your heart say?" she asked. D was always about the heart.

"My heart says I love you," I said.

"What does your heart say about this trade?"

"I don't want to leave Florida, but I don't want to let down my teammates. They're dying to play for the Dodgers."

"Have you prayed about it?" she asked.

"Not really."

"Give it a try, Gary. At times like this, I don't ask God for the answer, I just pray for clarity and understanding. I pray to do the right thing by everyone."

That prayer helped lead me to Los Angeles—at least, to discuss the issue.

When I got there, though, L.A. presumed I was accepting the trade and expected me to put on a uniform and play that night in Dodger Stadium against the Expos.

Not so fast.

First of all, I knew the Dodger organization was in a state of chaos. In March, the O'Malleys, who'd owned the team for over fifty years, had sold it to Fox Entertainment. Now Fox was scrambling to figure out how to run a ball club.

I went into a meeting with the general manager. He figured I was just there to sign. But I'd discussed the matter with my agent, and I had some thoughts of my own.

"What are they?" asked the GM.

"Why didn't you pay Piazza what he was worth? I'd love to play with Piazza. I think dumping Piazza is a mistake."

He was taken aback by my candor. He didn't expect this from a player. He thought my agent would do all my talking, but, in the end, I talk for myself.

"Piazza is ancient history, Gary," he said. "We're here to talk about you."

"To be honest," I said, "I have doubts about playing for a team that just traded away their best chance to win."

"We traded him for four winners," he said. "We think it's a great trade and we promise to build this team around other winners like you. We know you're coming off a championship. We know you got the fire in your belly, and we're not going to let that fire go out."

He sounded convincing, but I had other thoughts.

"As a businessman," I said, "I don't see this trade as equitable."

"What do you mean?" he asked. "We're paying you exactly what you'd get in Florida."

"Florida has no state income tax," I reminded him. "California does. Plus, real estate here is sky high. Buying a house here is another huge expense that I won't have if I stay in Florida. If you say this trade is equitable, make it equitable."

"What are you proposing?" he asked.

"Pay my taxes and buy me a house."

"That's ridiculous," he said.

"That's reasonable," I countered. "And more to the point, that's it. I'm happy to fly to St. Louis right now and rejoin the Marlins."

"We've never done this for a player before," he said. "This is unprecedented."

"I like breaking new ground," I said.

"In total dollars, how much additional money are we talking about?" he asked.

"Give me and my agent a couple of minutes and we'll tell you."

He left the room and we did some figuring. When the GM returned I faced him and said it plainly. "Six million."

His mouth dropped open.

"This is outrageous," he said.

"This is business," I reminded. "And this is only fair."

"Does it matter to you where the money comes from?" he asked.

"No."

"Give me an hour."

Three hours later, after marathon calls between the Dodgers and Marlins, the general manager came back with a counter-offer.

"Five million," he said. "Two and half paid to you by us. The other two and half paid to you by the Marlins. Do we have a deal?"

"We have a deal," I said, "only if I have the right to renegotiate in three years."

He hesitated. Then he shook his head no.

"Well, then, that's it. I'm off to St. Louis."

"Wait," he said, seeing I was serious. "You win."

. . .

I guess I did win, but I have to say that it didn't feel great. Not that I don't like it when negotiations conclude in my favor. I do. But when the Marlins won the Series, I regained that little-boy attitude of loving the game of baseball. Now it was back to reality and cold-blooded business. That's another game I've learned to play—the game of common sense. Common sense always leads me to one conclusion: If I'm a commodity, I'm getting maximum value for myself.

So just like that, my little world was turned on its head.

I was moving to Los Angeles.

And I wanted D to move with me.

WHO AM I?

In August 1998, my biological father died.

Though I hadn't seen the man for many years, I decided to attend the funeral out of respect. I knew it would be highly emotional for me, so I called DeLeon in Chicago.

"D," I said, "I know you have your job and everything, but it would mean a lot to me if you'd fly down to Florida and be with me for the funeral."

D didn't hesitate.

"I'll be there," she said.

That's when I knew that, despite her refusal to move out to L.A., and, as she put it, "play house," she really did care about me.

Thank God D was there.

It was rough.

It was rough when I got to the funeral home and saw my father's name: Marvin Johnson.

Marvin Johnson!

I'd always presumed that the man's name was Sheffield. I was his son, after all, wasn't I?

I went to my mother for the answer.

"Yes, you're his son," she said. "Marvin's the man I got pregnant by. He was your daddy."

"Then who's Sheffield?"

"Lindsay Sheffield is the man I was going to marry when I was pregnant with you by Marvin Johnson."

"And did you marry him?"

"No. We were going together, and we planned to get married, but you were born first. When you were born, I went to my mother for advice. 'Mama,' I asked, 'do I give Gary his daddy's name or the name of the man I'm going to marry?' "

"And what did Grandma say?"

"Your grandma didn't like your real dad. Called him a thug. I couldn't even speak his name in the house. 'Give Gary the name of the man you're going to marry,' she said. 'Don't burden him with the name of a man who doesn't care anything about him.' "

"So what happened to Lindsay Sheffield?"

"We never did have a chance to get married. Not long after you were born, he got killed."

"How?"

"During a robbery. He was trying to rob a nightclub and got shot. By then, though, you were officially Sheffield."

"Why didn't you tell me any of this before, Mama?"

"I didn't want to confuse you, baby. I didn't want to upset you."

I loved my mother. Loved her then. Love her now. But her story, true as it was and told to me at age twenty-nine, confused and upset me to the point where the inside of my head was whirling.

Fathers and sons have a special bond, whether they know each other or not. I had a deep bond with Harold Jones, the man who raised me. He's my dad and Mama's devoted husband. But when I was a kid I had an off-again on-again relationship with a man named Marvin, my biological dad. Now I'd learned that I carry the name of the man who was *going to be* my dad, a man I never even knew existed. Confusing things even more, at Marvin Johnson's funeral I learned of the existence of two children Marvin had had with other women. That meant I had a half-sister and a half-brother.

The bottom line was this:

My father's name is Johnson.

My mother's name is Jones.

My grandmother and grandfather's name is Gooden.

And I'm Sheffield, named for a man, killed in a robbery, whom I never knew.

I felt myself losing it.

Not that I'd admit vulnerability to anyone except D.

On the outside, I kept my cool, acted like everything was okay, but on the inside I was a mess. I kept asking myself—and asking DeLeon—"Who am I?"

"A child of God," she said. "A child of a God who loves you."

"But all these fathers," I said. "Three different fathers. It's a lot to think about."

"I know it is, Gary. You were thrown for a loop. But none of that changes the fact that you were raised by two people, Betty and Harold Jones, who love you. They were always there for you. Not all children can say that."

D was right. But I was still tripping. Thinking about Marvin Johnson, thinking about Lindsay Sheffield, thinking about how things would have turned out had Lindsay lived.

"You have a life to live," said D. "And there's no reason why this experience can't make you stronger. Besides, it's wonderful to learn you have a brother and sister."

I never got to know my sister, but my brother, a Marine, turned out to be a great guy.

D was right.

I had a life to live back in Los Angeles.

"But I still can't live it without you," I said to her. "Will you marry me, baby?"

The answer didn't come right away, but when it did, I had to thank God. God didn't close the deal for me, but I knew He had led the way.

BLEEDING
DODGER BLUE

Back in June, a month after the Dodgers signed me, the team was still in turmoil. They canned general manager Fred Claire and manager Bill Russell. Tommy Lasorda, long-time Dodger manager, was named the interim GM.

Lasorda's a Hollywood guy. Loves to hang out with the old-school stars. He'll talk your head off. No one likes the sound of his own voice more than Tommy. I wouldn't call him a brilliant strategist or a genius, but his enthusiasm for winning is contagious. He can pump you up and keep your spirits high. Tommy was the first guy I heard say, "I'm proud to say that I bleed Dodger blue."

Tommy took me aside when I arrived and began saying something I'd hear all the years I was in L.A.

"I'm a lifetime Dodger, Gary," he reminded me. "This team has never let me down and we're never going to let you down. I believe in the Dodgers and the Dodgers believe in you. I'm happy you're here because now you can finally relax. I see you as a lifetime Dodger, and I want you to start thinking the same way. Remember, we're more than a team. We're a family. We're *your* family."

Tommy was the champ of pep talk. He'd be so sincere you might see a tear in his eye. When he talked about his Dodgers, he'd choke on his words and you expected him to break down crying. At the time he said this stuff, he believed it. Maybe.

Meanwhile, the Dodger plan to win their 1998 division wasn't working. They thought the big competition would be the Giants. But it wasn't the Giants who were beating us; it was my old team, the Padres. And the player who gave the Padres the edge that year was the pitcher they'd obtained from the Marlins—Kevin Brown, who won eighteen games. It was the Yankees' year, though. The Yanks swept San Diego in the World Series and wound up winning more games than any team in major league history.

That first Dodger season, though, was a good one for me. The truth is that I put up big numbers every season I played in L.A. In 1998, in ninety games for the Dodgers, I hit .313, sixteen home runs, fifty-seven RBIs, and sixty-nine walks, more than anyone on the squad.

"We'll get 'em next year," said Lasorda. "Next year we're getting Kevin Brown."

That next year, according to one baseball analyst, I had the biggest season at bat of any Dodger since they moved from Brooklyn back in the fifties. I scored 103 runs, hit 101 RBIs and 34 homers, walked 101 times and wound up with a .301 average. I was flying. Maybe that's because I was beginning to believe that being a lifetime Dodger was a good thing. I was tired of being shoved around the leagues like a pawn on a chess board. The bigger reason, though, was DeLeon.

At the end of '98, she said the one word I'd been praying for. "Yes."

"HE WHO FINDS A WIFE FINDS A GOOD THING"

Proverbs 18:22

I was a changed man. I'm not saying that my relationship with God was what it should have been. I'm always working on that relationship. It's nothing that stays still. But I did realize, with D's help, that I'd better get out of the business of negotiating with God.

I saw that following a new path had taken me in a new direction. Until DeLeon, my view of women was immature. It was street. Women were there for my pleasure, or to be conquered, or to be subservient. That's the attitude of a kid growing up in the neighborhood. D changed my attitude.

If I wanted her, I'd have to wait. That in and of itself was something new. She wouldn't move in with me until we were married. And she wouldn't even consider marriage until she believed that I understood that her independence and career were as important as mine. Our relationship couldn't get in the way of her graduating from college. And it didn't. Our relationship couldn't stop her career as a singer and performer. And it didn't.

I'm not saying that all my macho ways disappeared overnight. We cling to our old ways. At least I did. And still do. But I could feel my heart changing and expanding. Sexism—like racism—is deeply incompatible with the love of God. On critical issues and at critical times, I learned that a man can be led by a woman. In fact, it was D who led me to a church in L.A. that helped firm up my faith.

The pastor, Bishop Noel Jones, reached me. He's a dynamic man who explains the Word with an equal measure of fire and insight. The man can preach. A friend calls him the John Coltrane of evangelical ministers because his sermons sound like jazz. His messages are emotional but also intellectual. Bishop likes to say that God is setting us up by putting us in circumstances where He reveals himself. Bishop calls it situations for revelations. Well, my situation with women—where I always got what I wanted but never got what I *really* wanted—was the situation that set me up for D.

To get her I had to change. To win her I had to lose my old self. To merit her I had to accept a new way of life. The strange part is that way of life was the one I'd always wanted: a happy home built on trust and devotion.

I'd finally learned to put first things first.

For example, asking D's dad for permission to marry his daughter. I went to Chicago for that express purpose. DeLeon and her mom said that this wouldn't be an easy meeting. I was determined to go ahead anyway.

I tried to keep it simple.

"I love your daughter with all my heart," I said. "I'll always honor and cherish her. I'll never disrespect her. And I'd like your blessing."

"Do you really think you're willing to settle down with just one woman?"

"Yes, sir."

"Do you think you're capable of being with just one woman?"

"Yes, sir."

"Given your profession and the temptations that men in your line of work face, don't you think you're fooling yourself?"

"No, I don't."

"So you understand the nature of commitment."

"I haven't always, Pastor Richards, but I do now."

"And you know it's not going to be easy."

"I know I have some rough edges. I think D can help me smooth out those edges. And in some ways, I can help her. But no matter what, you have my word that she'll be protected and cared for."

"I believe you, Gary," he finally said, "and I give you my blessing."

With that, we embraced.

D and her mom were amazed to see that we'd bonded. I think they were surprised to see that I'd humbled myself.

Humility doesn't come easy to me. Most professional athletes have problems with humility. Most professional athletes thrive on cockiness. Who even thinks about humility? But I found myself thinking about it all the time. I wanted humility because I wanted the Calmness. And I finally understood that there's no getting to God, there's no being *with* God, without humility.

Humility taught me that all I can do is tell my own story, leaving in all the confusions and contradictions. I don't have to figure it out. I just have to live it and follow God's loving light.

. . .

There was a beautiful light in the sky in the Bahamas when DeLeon and I married on February 4, 1998. Our grandmothers were there and so were our parents. We are each only children. Neither of us had married before. We wanted this ceremony small and intimate. We didn't want the attention of the outside world. We kept it secret.

The secret was out, though, when we got to the Bahamas and discovered that Oprah was doing her show from there. Because D had worked for Oprah over many years, Oprah and her crew knew her well. There was no way this could be a secret for long.

Because we wanted to celebrate and include our larger families and friends, we decided to have another ceremony a year later in Tampa. Bishop Jones flew in to officiate. Over five hundred people attended. D's friends Cece Winans and Yolanda Adams, famous gospel stars, sang. D sang a song she'd written for the occasion and had me in tears. I couldn't ask for any more.

DeLeon became close to my daughters, who often called her for advice. My sons and I grew closer. Things were coming together.

Los Angeles was looking good.

After my second season, though—the season where I put up record-breaking numbers—something happened that made me wonder.

Dodger ownership was shifting again.

MOVIE MOGULS AND
BASEBALL STARS

Just when you think you got the system beat, the system beats you.

Just as I was enjoying roaming the outfield in Dodger Stadium, just as I was cherishing the proud franchise memories associated with Jackie Robinson, Roy Campanella, and Don Newcombe, just as I was starting to relax into the simplicity and beauty of the game, the game changed.

The Dodgers' ownership was going through more chaos at the end of the 1999 season. That's the season in which the Diamondbacks, led by Randy Johnson, finished twenty-three games ahead of us. Our hitting was sharp—Adrian Beltre, Raul Mondesi, Eric Karros, Mark Grudzielanek, and I all had good years, but the team's pitching fell apart. Manager Davey Johnson switched me to left field, where I did fine—my fielding percentage was .972—but I sensed discontent in the front office all season long.

In October Bob Daley, who used to run Warner Brothers, bought into the team and, just like that, became the boss—managing partner, chairman, and CEO. I knew trouble was brewing.

I'm not saying that the guy didn't make a mint making movies. But *Batman* isn't baseball. Baseball requires another kind of mind.

"The guy was a big Brooklyn Dodgers fan when he was a kid," someone said, "and this is his life's dream—to run a team."

I thought of other owners I knew: rich guys looking for bigger toys. Their intentions might be good; their love of baseball might be real; but all of a sudden, because of their big bucks, they start buying and selling us like we're trading cards.

No matter, I started out the season like a house on fire. After eighty-one games, I was hitting .330 and had hammered twenty-seven home runs. We were in a race with the Giants, and during those early months I was red-hot.

In May, though, something happened that underlined the hypocrisy of major league baseball.

It happened in Wrigley Field.

I had good associations with Wrigley Field because that's where Sammy Sosa taught me how to tape a bat. I'd broken my finger and needed something between my skin and the wood. When Sammy saw what was happening, he offered to let me use his bats that were taped to protect against injuries.

"I don't want to use a bat to hit against you, Sammy," I said.

"Don't worry about it," said Sammy, who's about the nicest guy in baseball.

Not only did he let me use his bats; after the game he took the time to teach me how to tape them.

Cubs fans aren't as friendly to the opposing team as Sammy. Wrigley is the most traditional ballpark in America. When I say traditional, I mean the fans are right there on top of you. And the fans like to heckle. Sometimes I ignore them, and sometimes I heckle back. On this particular day, heckling wasn't on my mind; I'd just thrown my last warm-up toss to the center fielder and was waiting for the first hitter to step to the plate.

That's when I heard a commotion and looked down the right-field line. I saw my whole team running to the stands. I didn't know what was going on, but I got over there in a hurry. Apparently a fan had thrown things at one of our catchers, Chad Kreuter, in the bullpen. When Chad went into the stands after the guy, a ruckus broke out, and the team was going in to protect Chad. Soon as I saw what was going on, I thought — *What if the fans have weapons? What if they have knives?* So I reached into the stands, not to go after fans, but to pull my teammates back into the bullpen so they wouldn't get hurt.

That cost me—and other players—a two-game suspension.

That infuriated me. I was going in to make peace, not war. But baseball didn't listen.

Later that season, I made the All-Star team and went to Atlanta for the game. I demanded to see Frank Robinson, baseball's vice president for on-field operations. He's the one who handed out the suspensions.

He called me and joked, "Should I bring somebody with me?"

"Bring whoever you like," I said.

During the meeting, I painted an accurate picture of what had happened. All the photos and witnesses bore me out.

Frank listened and said, "Gary, I understand."

"Great," I said. "So you'll lift the suspensions?"

"Can't do that. The suspensions have already been issued. This office must be decisive."

"How about being right?" I asked. "Doesn't that count for anything?"

Apparently not, because the suspensions stood.

Talk about winning the battle and losing the war!

That 2000 season we lost the division to the Giants, but I wound up with 109 RBIs, forty-three homers, 109 walks, 105 runs, and a .325 average. I'd given the Dodgers just what they'd asked for.

That's why during the off-season when they floated rumors of trading me, I got mad.

Who wouldn't?

When the Dodgers initially traded for me, they gave me every indication that they considered me a franchise player. I'd moved my family to California. My daughter wanted to go to UCLA. DeLeon and I had started a life in Los Angeles. I had a minister in L.A. who was important to my spiritual life. I'd made the big adjustment and wanted to stay put.

From a strictly business point of view, I'd fulfilled my end of the bargain. The Dodgers had never fielded a player who put up numbers like this for three straight years.

All during the 2000 season the front office had been telling me they wanted me to retire a Dodger. That sounded great. That fit right in with my own plans. I bought the bit about bleeding Dodger blue. But I also knew that, given my performance, it was time to renegotiate. Besides, they were contractually obligated to do so. I'd insisted on that clause when I came over from Florida. No one could argue with that.

"The big man wants to meet with you about your future," said a Dodger executive. He was referring to Daley.

"Fine," I said. "I'll invite him to my house."

I told my agent about the meeting. He thought it was a good idea, but said we shouldn't discuss contracts. He told Daley the same thing, and, according to my agent, Daley agreed.

The next week, Daley came to my house and sat with me in my study.

First question came from him.

"Why do you want to be a lifetime Dodger?" he asked.

He asked the question aggressively, as if the idea had originally come from me.

"That's the idea I've been given ever since I got here," I said.

"Well, that was the old regime. This is the new one. I don't believe in lifetime guarantees," he announced. "I've negotiated contracts with the biggest stars in the world—movie stars, music stars—and no one gets a free ride."

What is this guy's problem? I was thinking to myself, but decided to try and keep it cool.

"Look," I said, "baseball isn't movies and baseball isn't music."

"I think I know something about baseball," he said.

His tone was getting to me. I couldn't help but say, "I'm not sure."

"And I'm not sure a new contract guaranteeing you anything is warranted," he said.

"Fine, then you'll have one unhappy Dodger."

"I can have you traded in two days."

"Great," I said. "I'll be waiting by the phone. You can't threaten me."

"You're the one doing the threatening," he claimed. "You're insinuating that if you're unhappy you won't perform."

"No, I'll go out there and do what I always do. I'll play my butt off, and I'll put up big numbers because that's how I'm made. But as far as you and the management go, don't expect me to give you the right time of day."

"And this is how you want to conduct a discussion about extending your contact?"

"I thought we weren't going to discuss my contract," I said.

"What else is there to discuss?" he asked.

"Nothing," I said, and got up and left the room. The meeting was over.

I stayed in L.A. a little while longer before going to Tampa for the winter. I was there watching TV when I heard reports that the Dodgers wanted to trade me for the Indians' Sandy Alomar.

I hit the roof. I gave statements to the press where I candidly offered my low opinion of Daley and Dodger management. I also said that my limited no-trade clause gave me veto power over a trade I didn't want—and I didn't want to go to Cleveland.

Daley and his boys fired back. They crucified me in the press. Called me selfish, spoiled, and impossible. Said nothing would make me happy, not even fabulous multimillion dollar contracts.

I hit back. Said I was tired of their cheap shots. Many players get millions of dollars. That doesn't mean we should be disrespected. Doesn't mean we should fall on our knees and thank these kindly owners for keeping us around.

It got bad. I killed the Cleveland deal and Daley was out to kill my reputation. He did a good job.

Meanwhile, I felt my agent had deserted me. When it came to explaining my position, he was nowhere to be found. I wound up doing my own talking. Maybe I should have sugarcoated my words, but I didn't. My words were salty, not sweet, and the escalation continued.

I fired my agent and suddenly other agents came from out of the woodwork. They tried to get to me every which way, including contacting DeLeon. When they did that, I struck them off my list forever. One agent with a strong reputation said he'd arrange a meeting and I could go from there. I agreed.

Daley's boys arrived before him. Everyone was optimistic.

"We're getting this thing worked out," they said.

But when Daley walked into the room, first thing he said to me was, "We don't have to give you anything we don't want to give you."

I got up and left.

Walking back to my car, the press were chasing after me. "What happened? What happened in there?" I didn't say a word.

One of Daley's guys caught up with me before I could pull away. He convinced me to come back and give them another chance. He swore that everyone was saying that they just had to sign me.

"Okay," I said, "I'll come back."

But when I went into the room, Daley was still raging about my attitude and how he didn't owe me a thing.

This time when I got up and left, I slammed the door behind me.

The Dodgers went to the press, where they continued their war of words. I hated that.

When I'd signed with the Marlins, it had been one of the biggest contracts in baseball history, yet no one knew about it until the day it happened. Florida didn't play me in the press and I didn't play them.

The Dodgers were just the opposite.

The Dodgers had nothing good to say about me, and I had nothing good to say about them.

The 2001 season was coming up. Management wasn't backing down, and neither was I.

How would this thing ever get resolved?

CHAOS AND
CALMNESS

When I came to Christ, I didn't know what to expect. All I knew was that something had changed inside me. I had to admit certain things about myself—the way I had used women, for instance, or the way I'd grown even more self-obsessed. When I met Terry Pendleton and later DeLeon— people whose peace of mind seemed so beautiful—I had to know where that peace of mind came from. They both pointed to God. More and more, I felt God pointing to me. The pointing didn't feel like punishment or retribution; it felt like love. It felt like God saying, *"Come to Me, rest in Me, give Me your burden, let Me guide you, let Me lead you into another life."*

I said yes. I entered into another life. I married D and com-mitted my heart to her and to God. I changed. I no longer felt that hole in my soul. I felt something else, a divine presence I really can't describe. I felt the Calmness. But if I expected the Calmness to chill out the rest of the world, man, was I wrong! The challenges of playing pro ball went on just like before. And just like before, I faced the same old stuff I'd always faced: the sweet poetry of a little boy's game played against the backdrop of cold-blooded business. That contradiction never went away. It's still there.

There was a powerful personality conflict. I didn't like Daley. He didn't like me. He thought I was trying to push him around. I knew he was trying to push me around. I wouldn't be pushed. And I wouldn't be quiet. If I thought the Dodgers were being run by someone who didn't know what he was doing, I said so.

The longer the nastiness went on, though, the more I was getting hurt. That's because their public relations skills were slick. I didn't have any public relations skills. If I had, maybe I could have avoided the whole mess. Instead the mess got messier.

During spring training, my new agent arranged another meeting and convinced me and Daley to attend.

I wasn't happy and neither was Daley.

I reminded him that when the Dodgers were trying to re-sign Chan Ho Park, an extremely effective pitcher, I knew it would cost them an arm and a leg. I'd offered to let the team defer some $30 million of my salary to facilitate keeping Park. I wanted Park signed because I wanted to win. I also reminded Daley that initially I'd been promised contract renegotiations after three seasons. Well, I'd just completed my third season.

Daley wasn't moved. "Tell you what," he said. "You wind up the 2001 season with the kind of numbers you produced in 2000, and I'll give you the deal you want."

I was tired of arguing.

I was completely confident that I could do just that, so I stuck out my hand and said, "You have my word."

Daley stuck out his hand and said the same. We shook hands.

"One other thing," he added. "I think you owe us a public apology. Your remarks have been unwarranted."

I was about to say, *"What about the way you've painted me as the villain?"* But I kept quiet. By then I knew the guy. It didn't take much to tick him off. If I really wanted to make peace, I'd have to be a man about it and swallow my pride. I remembered the proverb that says, "Pride goeth before destruction, and a haughty spirit before a fall."

"I'll publicly apologize," I promised.

And I did.

Opening day, 2001.

Despite many months of chaos, I was finally feeling the Calmness.

D and I drove to Dodger Stadium together. We sat in the car and prayed before I went to the locker room. Just prayed for God's peace. We both knew what I'd be facing: 53,000 fans who'd been reading stories about my greed. The Dodgers had spoon-fed those stories to the press, and the press, always looking for controversy, was happy to accommodate them. Tommy Lasorda, still on the Dodgers payroll as some sort of advisor, acted like he was on my side. But I knew otherwise. When I wasn't around, Lasorda joined the chorus of those calling me selfish. Lasorda was two-faced, and Lasorda was an expert at kissing up to those in power.

As the game started, I tried to put those thoughts behind me. I tried to remember the simple pledge I'd made to Daley. I was going to play my heart out.

First time up, I left the dugout and even as I got to the on-deck circle I could hear the boos. When I stepped up to the plate, the boos got crazy loud. I'd been booed before, but nothing like this. The fans were merciless. They were having a ball booing me.

Big Jamey Wright, a six-foot-six twenty-six-year-old right-hander, was on the mound.

He walked me. That didn't stop the boos.

Next at-bat I smacked a single. That still didn't stop the boos.

Bottom of the sixth. I came to bat with bases empty. Chan Ho Park and Wright were locked in a scoreless duel.

I stepped up to the plate. Boos louder than ever.

I stared down Wright. I waited for the right pitch. I got hold of one and airmailed it straight down center field, over the fence.

The boos suddenly turned to cheers.

I rounded third and as I touched homeplate, I pointed skyward.

That was the winning margin, 1–0.

One big hit at the right time and I was back in the fans' good graces.

That's baseball.

I had a good year, but the Dodgers fell to third place behind the Giants and Diamondbacks, who went on to beat the Yankees in a seven-game World Series.

I was disappointed that we hadn't made the playoffs, but I'd kept my word. I'd hit .311 for the year, had 100 RBIs, thirty-six homers, and ninety-four walks.

I had two more years to go on the six-year contract the Dodgers had bought from the Marlins. I put behind me the fact that the promise of renegotiating after three years had been broken. I'd made a new pledge with Daley, and now it was time to finally talk numbers.

"Call Daley and let's cut a deal," I told my agent.

An hour passed.

"He doesn't want to give you a deal," my agent reported. "He says you have two years left and that's it."

As a Christian, I'd made a vow not to curse. But I smashed that vow to bits.

Daley had given me his word.

The revolving door of Dodgers management was revolving faster than ever. The team was still in chaos.

The new GM called me.

"Things are different around here now, Sheffield," he said. "I don't have to give you anything."

Different lyrics, same song.

I told him that he didn't know me, and I didn't appreciate being talked to that way. "Besides," I added, "I don't have to do anything either."

"You have to play."

"I'm not going to play here, I can guarantee you that."

Right then and there, I knew it was over. I'd had it with the Dodgers and their Mickey Mouse management. Time to get traded.

Also, time to strategize: If my agent couldn't get me a deal with the Dodgers, what good was he? So I fired him and decided to arrange the trade myself.

I went public with my decision to get traded. That infuriated the Dodgers because they said that, since everyone knew I wanted out, they wouldn't get full value for me. My ex-agent said I'd never work out a trade.

"Watch me," I said.

I called back the general manager and said it plainly. "You don't want me. I don't want to be here. Trade me. Call the Braves. Frank Wren over there worked with Dave Dombrowski when I was with the Marlins. Wren knows the kind of player and the kind of guy I am. Wren will want me."

He did.

The deal went down quickly. The Dodgers traded me for Brian Jordan, Odalis Perez, and a minor league pitcher. The Braves picked up the two years remaining on my six-year contract, the first year at $9.5 million, the second for $11 million.

I was relieved to leave the Dodgers. It hadn't been easy for them or for me. I was also deeply disappointed. At age thirty-three I was still feeling that same little kid's brokenhearted blues when the truth became clear. The Dodgers don't bleed blue; they bleed green. All the talk about a lifetime commitment and contracts renegotiated in good faith went out the window. I couldn't help but be hurt. I thought of my grandfather and his feelings about the Dodgers. "They had the guts to bring Jackie Robinson on board back in 1947," he said, "when no other major league team would touch a black man. Gotta give 'em credit for that."

I did. I knew they had a proud history and I was proud to be part of it. I'm still proud to have the highest slugging percentage—.643—in team history. I gave it my all. If an owner like O'Malley had been around, maybe things would have been different. Without the insecure maneuverings of a bunch of guys who didn't know what they were doing, the story might have changed. Who knows?

All I knew was that I was moving on. Before the final trade came down, though, another event impacted my career and my attitude about not only baseball but life in general.

In the winter before the 2002 season, I accepted an invitation to work out with Barry Bonds in San Francisco.

BONDS

Doc and Darryl Strawberry used to talk about Barry Bonds all the time. They saw him, along with guys like Ken Griffey, Jr., as one of the game's great players. They said I belonged in that same category.

"No way," I said. "Bonds is in his own category."

I was flattered to be placed in his company, but I saw him as the better player.

When I went to L.A., I saw more of Barry because of the frequent Dodger-Giants games. I never knew him well, but we were friendly and he took a liking to me. He liked that I was outspoken.

After the 2001 season, just before my trade to the Braves, Barry invited me to San Francisco to train with him.

"Train with me, bro," Barry said, "and I'll take you to a new level. I can add years to your career. It's all about longevity."

My own training had evolved over the years. When I first went pro, I lived on fast food. Never paid much attention to what I ate. As the years went by, I started studying nutrition and saw the value of a balanced diet. Weight training became part of my routine. Personal trainers worked with me closely, and I listened to them. I learned. I began understanding how to gain strength by concentrating on different muscle groups. I began understanding the importance of intelligent training.

Now Barry was challenging me with a higher intensity. I liked challenges, so I accepted. Besides, I was curious to see Barry's plan.

I hated to leave my wife for any period of time, but DeLeon understood. I really didn't know what to expect, but, man, Bonds was something else!

Barry needed to be in control—that was the main thing. Most of us love control and work for it. Most of us get a little nervous when someone else is in charge. That's human nature. But Bonds took control to a whole new level. When I got there, that was the first thing I saw.

I was happy to live in a hotel.

"No," said Barry. "You'll live with me."

I wanted to rent a car.

"No way," said Barry. "I'll drive you wherever you need to go."

I wanted to tell Bonds about my usual training routine.

"I don't want to hear about it," said Barry. "I got the only routine that'll work for you."

Given Bonds's heavy-handed attitude, I was ready to leave after the first few days. I called D and said, "Baby, this boy is tripping. Never seen anyone so hooked on telling everyone what to do and when to do it."

"Well, Gary," said D, always a model of patience, "give it a chance. You came up there to learn, and maybe he'll ease up after a while."

He never eased up. It became clear that Barry was trying to test me; he wanted to see if I could take it.

The routine was hard-core:

1. Up at the crack of dawn and off to the Stanford football field for nonstop cardio. Laps. Hundred-yard sprints. Agility runs. Run for two hours.

2. Two hours in the weight room. Pull-downs, arm curls, bench press, the whole nine yards. "Go for the burn," said Barry.

3. After eating box lunches in Barry's car while driving to Pac Bell Park, back to cardio. That meant running the stairs for a good hour. Then down to the field for more sprints before

4. Going to the batting cage.

Barry had his own personal guy pitch batting practice to us, but the highlight of my day was when Barry's dad offered me tips. Bobby Bonds was great. His batting philosophy was right to the point: regardless of how you stand, hit to a straight line. Place your back foot in the direction of that line. That will balance your weight. It's not about looping your swing and dropping your back shoulder. It's about planting your feet in the direction you want to hit the ball. The rest will take care of itself.

Mr. Bonds was also big on swinging at strikes. That's all he talked about. Go for the strikes and pass on the bad pitches.

Until I met Mr. Bonds, walks would get me mad. I wanted to hit.

"Your thinking is wrong," said Mr. Bonds.

"How do you mean?" I asked.

"Let's say there are runners on first and third and you get walked."

"I don't like that," I said. "It means I've done nothing."

"Wrong. It means next time you come up they're going to pitch to you and that's when you'll do your damage. The point is this—don't look outside the strike zone. Stay in it. You'll make better contact. Better to let them work you deeper into the count, son. Take those walks. They'll improve your overall numbers."

Mr. Bonds was cool, but Barry was red-hot when it came to workouts. It was his way or the highway.

He told me he wanted a guy named Victor Conte, head of a company called BALCO, to give me vitamins based on my specific needs. I went along with it. Conte gave the vitamins to Greg Anderson, Barry's personal weight trainer, who gave them to me.

When Greg was supervising me, Barry would yell, "Give him another forty pounds on that bench press, Greg. He needs to lift more weight."

I decided we needed a break. Because Barry was hosting me in his house and paying for all this stuff, I wanted to do something for him. So I bought us first-class tickets to fly to Miami to see a fight. I arranged the whole thing—the airline, the limos, the hotel.

When my travel agent sent the itinerary to Barry's house in my name, Barry opened the envelope before showing it to me. He didn't like the airline, didn't like the time of the flight, didn't like the limo company or the hotel. He canceled everything and rearranged it all to suit himself.

My resentment was building. He was trying to make me feel like a child, totally dependent on him. I wanted to remind him that I was an adult, a professional athlete making $11 million a year. I could afford to pay my own way.

Things got even crazier because, during this same period, the Dodgers were in the process of trading me to Atlanta. Barry and I were working out in the gym when the Braves' Frank Wren called me.

"Get off the phone, Gary," Barry yelled. "We're working out."

"I'm talking to the Braves about the trade," I said.

Barry came over, took the phone out of my hand, put it to his mouth, and said, "We're busy here. If you wanna trade for Gary, do it. If not, don't bother us." With that, he hung up.

A few minutes later, my phone rang. Barry answered it. It was Wren.

"Leave Gary alone," said Barry. "If you call again, all we want to hear is that the trade's done."

Somehow the trade did get done.

Meanwhile, though, Barry's training methods were undoing me.

He was telling me I needed to do heavy squats, in spite of my recent knee surgery. "The squats will strengthen your knees."

Of course, *now* I know that was foolish. But at the time the macho, competitive part of me kicked in.

Barry thought he could break me. Well, if my uncle couldn't break me when I was a kid, Barry couldn't break me as a grown man.

I eased myself under the bar and did the squats with super-heavy weights.

I thought I could manage the weight. My legs have always been powerful. On the last set, though, as I gave it my all, I heard something pop.

My surgical stitches popped out.

"No problem," said Greg Anderson. "We'll get some cream that'll heal you up in a hurry."

I went to the doctor to check with him. My understanding was that the cream was not that different from the Neosporin you buy at Rite Aid. Only it worked quicker.

It did work fast. It healed me in about a week.

Meanwhile, DeLeon was telling me I needed to come home. She didn't like the way Barry was treating me. She thought he was doing more harm than good. For dumb macho reasons, though, I was determined to stick it out. But I started doing things more on my own terms. I started sleeping later. Barry didn't like that. He hated waiting for anyone. Then one morning he left for the workout without me.

That was rude, but I figured I could find my own way to the stadium.

I caught up with him around 8 A.M. He was down on the field talking to some reporters.

"Let's do sprints," he said to me.

"I gotta take it easy today," I said. "My knees are still aching."

With the reporters listening, Bonds started making fun of me. He said that this hard training was too much for me. He was angry that I didn't get out of bed when he told me to. His revenge was to make a bunch of jokes at my expense.

Far as I was concerned, that was it.

I didn't say a word. Didn't argue. Didn't defend myself. I just left. Hopped a plane back to Tampa, where D was waiting for me.

Never said another word to Barry.

Still haven't.

But Bonds was determined to keep bad-mouthing me. He belittled me to the media and even complained that I messed up his eighty-thousand-dollar car by dropping crumbs on the floor while eating lunch. He insinuated that I'd been mooching off him.

When the media ran to me for a rebuttal, all I said was "God bless Barry."

I'm still saying "God bless Barry."

RAGE OVER 'ROIDS

Barry was still furious that I'd left his personal training camp. He told BALCO to send me a bill for the vitamins. No problem. DeLeon wrote them a check for about four hundred dollars.

That check linked me to BALCO.

Later some people claimed the cream contained steroids. I don't know if it did.

I had no interest in steroids. I didn't need them, and I didn't want them.

I *never* wanted them. From the get-go, I've frequently mouthed off about their negative impact on the game.

I knew what was happening. Everyone did.

The 1994 players' strike had made fans angry. The World Series was canceled. After that, attendance was down. But when

McGwire started the home run mania, attendance came back. The owners understood that the sudden spike in homers wasn't accidental. All baseball knew it. But baseball is run on money, and home runs meant money. Baseball turned a blind eye.

I didn't.

I was accurately quoted as saying that we were giving the public a false picture of the game. I asked the Commissioner to investigate. He paid no attention to me. I complained that players were banging home runs in August and September like it was April and May. They were showing no fatigue. Something wasn't right.

My dad's a bodybuilder. My whole life I've been taught to train the hard way. I believe in *earning* strength, not buying it. My grandfather raised me old school: In baseball, you work for whatever you get.

I've never touched a strength-building steroid in my life—and never will. The proof is in the pictures and my stats.

Look at pictures of my body before I trained with Bonds and after. There's no difference. I look the same. I am the same. If you compare my numbers before I trained with Bonds and after, there's no spike. If anything, there's a drop-off.

In 2001 with the Dodgers—the year before I trained with Bonds—I hit thirty-six home runs with a slugging percentage of .583. In 2002 with the Braves—the year *after* I trained with Bonds—I hit twenty-five home runs with a slugging percentage of .512. My single biggest home run year was back in 2000 when I connected for forty-three. After 2003, I enjoyed another three years of hitting thirty homers or more. But I've never again hit forty in a single season.

When I was subpoenaed to testify about steroids before a grand jury, I was in and out of there in ten minutes.

I got right to the point.

"I applied this cream to my knees," I told them. "I didn't

know it was steroids. Whatever it was, it didn't make me stronger."

I didn't testify against players because I've never seen another player take steroids. I knew players did—everyone knew it—but I had no firsthand knowledge.

Over the years, I kept voicing my opinion to anyone who'd listen:

"This isn't an easy game. Just ask Michael Jordan. Hitting a baseball might be the hardest thing in sports. I've been training hard my whole life. My whole life I've been driven to be a winner. So I want a level playing field. I don't want anyone having an unfair advantage over me. I don't cheat, and I don't want anyone else cheating."

End of story.

TAKE ME
TO THE RIVER

My mother's people are from Georgia, so maybe that's why when I got to Atlanta, I felt a spirit saying, "Take me to the river. Get baptized, Gary."

In the days before our people had money to build baptismal fonts, they went to the river. The river stood for the cleansing power of Christ. When you went there, you submitted to His will. You gave Him your life.

I loved that idea, but I'd also been resisting it—the idea of surrendering entirely to God. I wanted to hold on to control. Inside me were the last vestiges of skepticism. But after going through what I went through with Barry, I saw how an overly controlling nature will mess up a man. It will make you mean and have you believing you're some kind of god. Surrendering to a will other than our own isn't easy, especially when that will is shrouded in mystery. But if I were to grow spiritually, I understood that it was absolutely necessary.

I wasn't looking for miracles. I didn't think that the baptismal waters would wash all my flaws away. I knew that I was, and am, a work in progress. But to give that work over to God, rather than rely on my own willpower, looked like the right move.

When Jesus asked John the Baptist to baptize Him, He was following his Father's will. He was demonstrating humility. A public demonstration of my own humility—a quality I both desire and resist—could only do me good.

So, symbolically speaking, I went to the river. I submitted. I was submerged. I said to God, "I'm Yours. Teach me. Grow me. Live in my heart."

I still say that every day.

But on the day of my baptism, a beautiful day when I felt closer to Christ than ever before, I do have to admit one thing:

After spending the day embracing humility, I did something that showed me my humility was still unsteady. In the game that night, an umpire's call infuriated me.

I was safe at second by a mile when he called me out. My slide was way under the tag. The ump had to be blind.

I called him a name. Then another.

God had to be laughing, because on the same day that I was baptized in His holy name, I was thrown out of the game!

Let the church say, "Amen."

SHEF'S CHEFS

Looking back, I see my two years in Atlanta as a beautiful time. I was relaxed. Life was simpler. And I could finally concentrate on my family. It was Atlanta where DeLeon gave birth to our first son, Jaden. With the craziness of the Dodgers behind me, Atlanta became the first place where I could stop and appreciate the things that counted most: a loving wife, loving children, and that Calmness that comes with faith.

The big business of baseball would get even bigger. The back-room wheeling and dealing would get crazier, the subtle (and not so subtle) racism would continue; the press would depict me any way it pleased them. But none of that mattered the way it used to matter.

Calmness overwhelmed the old chaos.

Atlanta was a bridge between L.A. and New York. I say that

because in the back of my mind I still hadn't forgotten what I'd witnessed when Doc was in the World Series with the Mets. I still believed New York was the roughest, toughest, and most exciting baseball town. I still saw New York as the ultimate. But before trying for New York, I also knew I needed time to gather my resources—mental, emotional, and spiritual. Atlanta was the perfect place to do that. I could play out the last two years of my six-year contract with the Braves. The money was great, the fans were welcoming and warm, and the coach was the best.

I loved Bobby Cox. Bobby was another of those fine father figures who gave his players complete respect and support. He had a gift for encouraging you while staying out of the way and letting you play your game. For Bobby, it was always a game first and a business second. He knew it was about staying loose and having fun. At age sixty-two, he'd be out there on the diamond during practice, fielding grounders like he was thirty. I never heard Bobby say a negative word about a player. If something went wrong during a game, he'd take the blame. He protected his players no matter what. Even better, the man didn't have a racist bone in his body. Bobby Cox was all heart.

Compared to the Hollywood hypocrisy of L.A. or the hardcore street vibe of New York, Atlanta was laid-back. Atlanta was country folk, and I loved them. It felt good being appreciated again.

"We appreciate your talent," Cox said to me when I first came over, "and I'd like to know what position you'd prefer to play."

The question floored me. No manager had ever asked me where I wanted to play. The two other Braves outfielders—Chipper Jones and Andruw Jones—were superstars. Yet here Bobby was deferring to me.

"Tell you what," I said. "I'd rather know where Chipper is most comfortable."

"Chipper prefers left."

"Then I'll take right."

And that was that.

For two years, we had the most formidable outfield in either league. Chipper, Andruw, and I operated like a unit. We were three, but we played like one. I've never felt so comfortable in the field. It was like being a kid again.

Our offense was as good as our defense. In addition to Chipper and Andruw, we had Rafael Furcal and Javy Lopez. Plus powerful pitching: Greg Maddux, Tom Glavine, Kevin Millwood, and John Smoltz.

The thing that moved me most, though, was a fan club called Shef's Chefs. One day I looked in the stands and saw all these people wearing big white chef's hats. They waved at me and started yelling, "You're our man, Shef. You're the one, baby." This was a first for me, and I found myself all choked up. After what I'd seen in Milwaukee and L.A., where many fans would turn on you on in a heartbeat, this display of affection was something else. These people really believed in me.

That belief came in handy when I fell into a serious slump early in the season. That same belief helped me find my stride. Those fans never did give up on me. I wound up with a good year—hit .307 and twenty-five home runs. My twenty-three game-winning RBIs led the National League. We walked away with our division and faced the Giants in the play-offs. That meant facing Bonds.

Bonds had had a sensational year. He'd hit .370 and forty-six home runs. He'd won his fifth MVP award and the second in a row. But Barry had never made it past the first round in the play-offs, and we were determined he never would.

In the opening game at Turner Field I homered, but the Giants outscored us 8–5. We came back to win the next two games and, going into game 4, we were only a victory away from the National League championship series.

San Francisco clobbered us in game 4, 10–2, setting up a series-deciding game 5 on our home field.

I was so gung-ho on helping my team make it to the World Series, I lost my sense of relaxation. After that first game, I failed to hit for the rest of the series and wound up with a .083 post-season average. Game five belonged to Bonds. He homered and scored twice. The Giants won 8–3. San Francisco would eventually lose that year to the Angels in the World Series, but that didn't diminish the sting of our loss.

The next year, 2003, my fifteenth season as a pro, was one of my best. I was happy in all aspects of life—my marriage was beautiful, and my relationships with my children were improving. I still struggled with old issues, among them how to be a positive influence for my kids when their lives had, from time to time, been disconnected from mine. I always hung in there with them. My children would never lack for material comfort. I also stressed education and tried, as best I could, to teach them that independence and self-reliance are vital to leading happy, productive lives.

D and I had joined the Without Walls International Church in Tampa, where Randy and Paula White, gifted ministers who happen to be white, lead a multiethnic congregation under a banner of love and loving community service. When Randy and Paula talk about tearing down the walls of racism and poverty, they do more than talk. They act. "The church," they say, "isn't a museum for saints, but a hospital where the wounded come to be restored and healed." Much of my own healing has come through their teaching.

But as my ministers like to say, "Without Walls is the perfect church for people who aren't perfect." In my professional life, I saw that again in 2003.

There were many moments during that season when I felt that little-boy wonder of playing ball. Running out to right field to take my position, I'd think: *This is the Atlanta Braves, the team for which my grandfather's idol, Hank Aaron, set the all-time home run record. This is a dream come true. If only Grandpa could see me now!*

When we won our division again, I was ready to romp. Andruw Jones, Marcus Giles, and Javy Lopez had huge years. I wound up hitting .330 and knocked in 132 RBIs. I had the most hits of my career—190—and an on-base percentage of .419. I was certain I could propel the Braves past the Cubs in the division series, win the pennant, and bring Atlanta its first World Series since 1995.

So what did I do? I tried too hard and wound up going two for fourteen. My .143 didn't do much to help the team, and the Cubs—who went on to lose the pennant to the Marlins, eventual World Series winners over the Yanks—beat us in five.

You'd think that by age thirty-four I would have learned how to escape my ego at play-off time. But the raw truth is that my ego grips me hard. The cocky side of my nature is easily excited. I can get into the mind space of saying, *I'll carry this team on my back; I'll lead them to victory; I'll do what no one has ever done.* That pulls me out of the moment, out of the zone. It gets me overeager and overstimulated, which messes up my timing. You could say that I sometimes have the problem of trying to *play* God rather than listen to him.

Despite my disappointing play-off performances, though, I still cherished my two years in Atlanta. They were among the best in my career. I knew, though, that playing out the remainder of my time and moving into the free agent market would set me up for a big move. I saw that move as the culmination of my business career.

My thinking was clear: If I'm going to play the business game, I'm going to play to win. And when it comes to baseball, there's no bigger business than the New York Yankees.

I knew George Steinbrenner was a shrewd operator, but I also had confidence in my own shrewdness.

Could I deal with Steinbrenner? Could he deal with me?

We'd have to see.

PINSTRIPES

God blessed me with a particular talent. I believe with all my heart that all God's children have been granted talent. Some discover that talent early, some later. In my case, my talent proved to have commercial value. At an early age, that both excited and confused me. I knew I was privileged, but I also learned I was part of a system—a business culture—in which only the strongest and smartest survive.

I realize that fans have a special relationship to baseball. They love the sport. It represents their own childhood—a time in their life when the world was simpler. Fathers and mothers take their little boys and girls to games, just the way they were taken to games by their folks. A beautiful innocence surrounds baseball. Fans want their heroes to be equally in love with the game. They want their heroes to play out of passion, not out of greed or gain.

I understand that. I understand how a husband who works hard all week at construction or a wife worried about doctors' bills could easily resent a baseball player bitching about making $5 million instead of $10 million. I'm aware that these are quality problems that most people wish they could face.

But the truth is that we all live inside our different cultures. And within those cultures are rules and regulations, restrictions and expectations.

In terms of pure moneymaking, it's great to be part of the culture of Major League Baseball in the twenty-first century. After decades of nasty exploitation, owners have finally been forced to pay players what they're worth. They've been forced to admit that a powerful player results in powerful profits.

I never forget—not for a single day—that I'm fortunate to have come up in an era when premier players can literally make a fortune. I don't take it for granted. I know I was born at a good time.

But I also know that, being part of this system, I have a choice: I can passively accept what it brings me, or I can challenge it. As a player, I'm aggressive. That's me. And, over the course of two decades, if I've also become an aggressive businessman, I can't apologize. That's also me.

After Los Angeles, I had my eye on the Yankees. Atlanta was a wonderful stop in between the two biggest markets in America. But deep down I knew that Atlanta wasn't prepared to pay what it would cost to buy me on the free agent market.

I felt free in all ways. I didn't have an obligation to any team. I didn't have an agent. Instead, I had an advisor, Rufus Williams. I met Rufus through DeLeon, who knew him when she worked for Oprah. A CPA, Rufus had been chief financial officer, controller, and vice president for financial planning and strategic development for Oprah's HARPO Entertainment Group. He also managed Oprah's philanthropic projects and was appointed by

Mayor Richard Daley to serve on the Chicago Board of Education.

When it comes to numbers and sound money advice, Rufus is brilliant. Beyond his brilliance, though, he doesn't carry the baggage of so many fast-talking, self-serving agents. He understands and respects my own ability to get in there and negotiate on my own behalf. He encourages that, but he also makes certain to school me in sophisticated finance. He corrects me when I'm wrong.

With Rufus watching my back, I felt sure I could do as well, if not better, than the agents I'd been observing for so many years.

Atlanta started the ball rolling, claiming they really wanted to sign me. They offered me $10 million a year for three years.

I know that sounds great, but I was already making over $11 million. And I was coming off a .330 average and thirty-nine home runs.

Did it make sense to take a pay cut?

I didn't think so.

At the same time, other teams started weighing in with more or less the same yearly salary—about $10 million. Like any player, I knew that collusion occurs when general managers discuss salary offers among themselves. That's illegal. It's also maddening, because it limits a player's ability to use the free-agent business model. I couldn't prove collusion, but it sure crossed my mind.

I had two goals: to overcome the obstacles created by possible collusion and realize my maximum worth; and to finally play on the biggest stage of all, Yankee Stadium. If I couldn't achieve both goals, maybe I could at least achieve one.

The setting was Tampa in the winter—my home turf. I was counting on Tampa to give me home-field advantage. But Tampa is also winter home to George Steinbrenner and the location of the Yankees' spring training.

From the very beginning, I knew I had to think like an agent, not a player. That meant suppressing my feelings—good or bad—for a person I was dealing with, or my excitement at playing for a certain team, and focusing on the numbers.

My uncle Dwight, meanwhile, had retired in 2001. He was still struggling with his demons, but had found work in the Yankees front office. Steinbrenner had helped Doc before, and he was helping him now. Doc was also helping me by whispering in George's ear, "Gary's great. Compared to Vladimir Guerrero"— my main competitor in the free-agent free-for-all—"Gary's your best bet." "But Gary's hard to handle," Steinbrenner told Doc. "I can handle him," Doc assured. "I'm his uncle."

Things started off badly.

Brian Cashman, the Yankees' general manager, offered me $4 million a year for two years. I took that as an insult and told them, "Thanks but no thanks. You aren't even close."

"They aren't even serious," I told Doc.

"Don't worry, Bug. That's just how George plays. He has his man Cashman come in low and then George beefs it up. George likes to be the hero and cut the deal himself. It'll be all right. Trust me."

I love my uncle, but I also knew that Doc was indebted to Steinbrenner in ways I wasn't. To me, Steinbrenner wasn't a lifesaver and a kindly gentleman. He was the same as all the owners: a ruthless businessman. I believed Doc when he said I'd ultimately have to deal with the boss himself, but that would have to happen on *my* terms, not his.

Meanwhile, the Braves continued to court me. The execs wanted to meet with me in person. Fine, I said, come to Tampa.

Because I suspected collusion was going on, I figured they wouldn't go over $10 million. But since I couldn't be sure that Steinbrenner would come through, there was no reason not to listen to Atlanta—as long as I could arrange the meeting.

I did. I decided on Malios, a Tampa restaurant filled with Yankees memorabilia. Steinbrenner had a private room at Malios where he lunched every day. I wanted him to see me hanging out with Atlanta management, and I wanted Atlanta management to see George greeting me.

When the Braves execs and I sat down, I chose a table Steinbrenner would have to pass by. I also told the waiter to take a long time between courses. George hadn't arrived yet, and timing was crucial.

We went from appetizers to salads. No Steinbrenner. Entrees arrived, and still no George. As predicted, Atlanta's offer stayed at $10 million. They had all kinds of reasons why I should stay, but the reasons were emotional, not monetary. My focus was on monetary incentives.

Finally, during dessert, George showed up.

He came by the table. Big smile. Handshakes all around. Slaps on the back. "Great seeing you, Gary," he said.

The Atlanta bigwigs saw what was happening. They felt George's interest in me. They upped their offer of $10 million a year from three years to four. "Guaranteed $40 million," they said.

"Pay me $39 million for three years," I countered, "and I'll consider it."

They passed, then paid the bill and left.

I lingered behind.

Once they were gone, I went into Steinbrenner's room.

"Excuse me, George," I said, "but I think we should talk—man to man."

"Agree," said Steinbrenner. "We'll talk tomorrow. Doc will know where to find me."

Next day Doc and I found George in the locker room at Legends Field, the Yankees' spring training ballpark in Tampa.

"First thing," said Steinbrenner, pointing to the beard I'd just grown. "You're gonna have to cut off that thing."

"I don't work for you yet, George," I said.

"Let's get down to brass tacks, Gary," he said. "I'm prepared to offer you $10 million a year for three years."

"You and everyone else," I said. "I have this theory that you and your owner friends got together and decided there was a right number for me. Isn't that collusion?"

Steinbrenner denied it.

I figured he would.

"That's as good as you're going to get," he claimed.

I knew he was bluffing.

"You're overpaying half your team," I said, "and you expect me to take a cut from what I made last year? Doesn't make sense, George. Plus, I can do whatever anyone else on your team can do. Maybe more."

I was confident. I was cocky. I kept pointing to my history. "Look at my long record," I said. "My numbers speak for themselves. At this point in my career, I'm beyond having to prove myself."

"You know, Gary," said George, "you're right. You are worth it. Plus, I'd love to see you in pinstripes when you hit your five hundredth home run. I'll pay you the $13 million a year you want for three years, but only if you give me a fourth-year option."

"Deal."

"Deal," Steinbrenner confirmed. "Meet me in my office tomorrow and we'll sign the papers."

We shook hands, and I left elated.

I'd done it.

I'd achieved both goals:

I'd broken through what seemed like collusion and got my $39 million; and I was going to wind up my career with the most prestigious team in all sports.

Or was I?

Next day Doc and I showed up at Steinbrenner's private office overlooking home plate at Legends Field.

The office gave off a heavy corporate vibe: *This is where the boss rules.*

Steinbrenner sat at the end of a huge conference table. On the wall behind him was a blackboard. I could feel his impatience. So could his execs, who kept nervously looking at him and the numbers on the blackboard.

First year: $8.5 million; $4.5 million in arrears.

Second year: $8.5 million; $4.5 million in arrears.

Third year: $8.5 million; $4.5 million in arrears.

Option year: $8.5 million; $4.5 million in arrears

"What is this?" I asked Steinbrenner.

"Your deal."

"This isn't the deal we agreed on yesterday."

"Yes, it is."

"Don't play me, George," I said. "Just because I'm acting as my own agent doesn't mean I'm naive. You didn't say anything about putting money in arrears. Why should I defer salary when no one else on your team is doing that? Besides, if I do agree to deferrals, shouldn't I be earning interest on that money?"

"I'll make it up to you," Steinbrenner promised. "I'll get you sponsorship deals."

"I'll get myself another deal with another team," I said.

And with that I got up.

"Where's he going, Doc?" George said.

"Don't worry, George," my uncle replied.

George turned red as I slammed the door behind me.

Doc followed me outside.

"You can't do this, Bug," he said. "I promised George I'd see this thing through."

"Look, Doc," I said, "I love you like a brother. I love you with all my heart. But this is business, and I've got to conduct it in my own way."

I kept walking.

Doc called later that day and said George wanted another meeting. He'd have a better explanation for the deal and break it down in clear, concise terms. Doc pressed me to give George another chance.

I relented. But this time I brought in Rufus Williams. I wanted him to see the numbers. Something might get by me, but nothing gets by Rufus.

When I walked into the meeting room, the lights were off. Steinbrenner's execs were sitting in the dark.

"Why?" I asked Doc.

"The boss is angry at them because your deal isn't done yet."

Someone switched on the lights and a few minutes later the boss walked in.

"Who's he?" George asked, pointing to Rufus.

I introduced Rufus Williams, rattling off his credentials.

Steinbrenner balked.

"He can't stay in here," he said.

"Why not?" I asked.

"Because this deal is between you and me. You didn't say anything about bringing an advisor, agent, or manager. If he doesn't leave, I don't deal."

I thought about it for a second. "Rufus," I said, "please wait outside. This won't take long."

It didn't take long. George just wanted to seal the deal. When it comes to deals, he has no patience. But when Steinbrenner offered the same deal as the day before, I walked out again. This time I slammed the door even harder.

Doc came after me again.

"It's no use, Dwight," I said. "I don't need this man. The language on this contract favors him. Everything favors him. I'd rather sit home and watch TV next year than play under those terms."

Doc must have said some things to George, because George got back to me and Rufus.

George said he'd change the language if I'd agree to the deferrals. I said I'd agree to the deferrals if the Yankees paid interest on them. He said he'd take care of the deferral interest after the season.

I finally relented.

George restated his pledge to get me sponsorships—which, by the way, he never honored.

The truth was that I wanted to play in New York and nowhere else. I had to get New York out of my system.

"I'm going to kill for your team, George," I said. "I'm going to prove that I'm worth every penny you're paying me."

That year, 2004, I finished second place in the MVP voting to Vladimir Guerrero, with some writers and fans arguing that I should have won.

I kept my word.

THE CALMNESS: REVISITED

Some friends said to me, "Gary, you talk about finding God. You talk about the love that you have in your heart for Christ. You say all these things, but we still see you arguing with ownership and doing all the things you've always done. How come?"

"Loving the Lord," I said, "doesn't mean you turn into a monk. Loving the Lord doesn't mean that the negatives leave you alone. When the negatives hit, you need that Calmness more than ever."

Early in our marriage, the press thought they'd found a negative, and they went after it with a vengeance.

Here's the whole story:

Before we married, DeLeon told me that as an eighteen-year-old she'd dated R. Kelly, an R&B singer.

That revelation didn't bother me. How could it? I'd had tons of relationships. Whatever happened between her and an old boyfriend was in her past. Her present and future were with me and our family.

Case closed.

But the case was reopened when, while we were still living in Atlanta, people began calling DeLeon, talking about a videotape with her and R. Kelly. They were demanding millions in hush money. DeLeon was pregnant with Jaden and emotionally at the most vulnerable point in her life. The blackmailers contacted her—not me—because they wrongfully presumed that I didn't know that she'd dated Kelly.

D immediately did the right thing. She contacted the FBI, who started monitoring her calls.

Fortunately, the blackmailers went away.

Our beautiful son was born and we thought the issue was dead.

Two years passed. I'd just completed my first year with the Yankees. D and I were chilling out in Mexico when Rufus Williams called.

"Are you sitting down?" he asked us.

We sat down.

Another blackmailer had come out of the woodwork. This time it was a man calling himself a preacher. If D would join his ministry, employ him as her spiritual counselor, and give him money, he'd keep quiet. He also implied that D had continued dating R. Kelly after our marriage, a bold-faced lie.

Our course of action was clear.

"Call the FBI," we told Rufus. "Let's put this guy behind bars."

Both D and I understood the implications of what we were doing: The minute this jack-leg preacher was caught, news of D's former relationship with R. Kelly would hit the papers.

"The papers will have a field day with this," said D. "Does that bother you, Gary?"

"No," I said. "I just want to bury this jerk who thinks he can hold us up."

The FBI advised Rufus to ask the blackmailer for a meeting. Rufus did just that. Rufus attended the meeting wearing an FBI wire. The blackmailer laid it all out. He told Rufus just what he'd been telling D. He convicted himself. Caught red-handed, he went to jail.

The press ran with the story. They really played it up, put it in headlines. They camped out around our house in suburban New Jersey for days. They insinuated things about DeLeon that weren't true.

It came down to this: We wouldn't be intimidated and we wouldn't be blackmailed. If the world found out that D had dated a celebrity when she was eighteen, so be it.

I stood behind her all the way.

And I was never so proud of anyone when, in spite of the negative press, D refused to crumble.

Other women, wanting to protect their reputation at any cost, might have suggested paying a blackmailer. Not DeLeon. She said, "My faith is in God. I'm walking through this with my head held high."

I'm not saying that the false news reports didn't give us restless nights and bad days. I was the new kid on the block in New York, and this wasn't exactly what D and I had foreseen as a welcoming party. We struggled with our anger and resentment.

We reacted as most people would react—sometimes tense, sometimes confused. But we were comforted by the absolute knowledge that God's love for us and His blessing of our marriage were indestructible. The Calmness pointed to the Proverbs where it says, "Weeping may endure for a night, but joy comes in the morning."

Morning came.

Joy arrived.

Faith saw us through.

THE CORPORATION

The Yankees' pinstripes are famous around the world. They're famous because they're distinctive and worn by the most successful team in the history of sports. You have to respect those pinstripes. I did and do. In fact, I worked hard to get to wear them. And I wore them with pride.

But as I got into the Yankees culture that first year, I also saw that the pinstripes were apt symbols for another reason. I thought of high-priced execs who wear pinstriped suits. I began seeing the Yankees not so much as a baseball culture, but as a business culture. If Los Angeles was hyped-up Hollywood and Atlanta kicked-back country, New York was cold-blooded corporate. I couldn't help but see the Yanks as the Corporation.

When you go to work at Yankee Stadium, it's like going to an office. The Yankees are an efficient, no-nonsense profit-making machine.

Early on, it became clear that the Corporation had an awfully cozy relationship with the press. That was also the case with the Dodgers. But the Yankees took it to another level. Certain people had access to the dressing room while others didn't. Even more important, certain management attitudes were conveyed to certain media when management needed to shore up their positions.

Watching all this, I went into a shell. I missed Chipper and Andruw something fierce. But I wanted to adjust. I wanted to kick back and watch it all unfold. After all, the 2004 Yankees were loaded with big-name talent—Hideki Matsui, Jason Giambi, Derek Jeter, A-Rod, Bernie Williams, Kevin Brown, Mike Mussina. These guys were all great. I loved them. And I got along with them. I was content just to be one name among many. I wasn't looking to stand out. I was just looking to quietly do my job.

Manager Joe Torre said very little to me. He was an enigma. His thing was basically, "Shef, you're batting number five." I hadn't hit fifth before; my usual spot was third, but five was fine with me.

What wasn't fine, though, was the way Torre talked to the press. He kept lamenting how his heart was set on getting Vladimir Guerrero, who'd gone with the Angels. The implication was that Torre would rather have Guerrero than me. Meanwhile, I was having a lousy April at bat, and every time I heard Torre praising Vladimir, I got mad.

Things came to a head in May. We were in Baltimore when I decided to confront Joe before the game.

I went to his office and said, "I'm tired of hearing you talk about how much you love Guerrero. That disrespects me."

"I know you're struggling, Gary, and I know that weighs on you."

"I've struggled before, Joe," I said, "and I'll struggle again. It's not the struggling that bothers me. It's that you haven't really said a word to me about anything. Feels like when you look at me, you'd rather be looking at Guerrero."

"I only made those comments about Vladimir because he's seven years younger than you."

"That doesn't make any difference."

Then he added, "I also know that getting used to American League pitching can take a while."

"That doesn't make any difference either. Look, when I go out on the field, that's my house. Any field. Any league. That's where I live. That's where I'm comfortable. And in my house I can dominate any time I decide to."

"That's an arrogant statement, Gary."

"Watch me back it up."

That day I went four for five and drove in six runs.

Wasn't long before I was batting third.

Wasn't long before Torre started calling me out during team meetings.

I didn't like that.

It happened in St. Louis.

I went down on one knee to field a hit and try to fool Larry Walker, a crafty base runner. I have a strong arm and can usually make an accurate throw, even when I'm not standing. But this time my release was too sudden and Walker slid safely into second.

The play didn't cost us the game, but we lost anyway. There were a number of dropped balls that day, and Torre decided to have a closed-door meeting.

"What kind of play was that, Sheffield?" he asked, using my throw as an example of the kind of sloppy ball the Yanks were playing.

I wanted to say, *How about all those errors that had nothing to do with me?* but I kept my mouth shut.

That day I told D the story.

"He knows you're strong," she said, "and that you can take it. He's just using you in a good way to get to the other players. He sees you as a leader."

D calmed me down, but when I got to the ballpark the next day, I saw big headlines in the New York papers about how Torre had scolded Sheffield.

I was fuming.

I was also told I wouldn't be playing that day.

Fine. I stretched out on a couch in the clubhouse.

Around the sixth inning, bench coach Joe Girardi came in and said, "Shef, Torre wants you in."

"Torre gave me the day off."

"Torre changed his mind," said Girardi as he headed back to the dugout.

I slowly went to get my glove. By the time I was ready to leave the clubhouse, though, Girardi was back.

"Torre said never mind."

Next day Torre called me to his office.

We had it out.

I told him I was furious that he'd called me out—and furious that the story had gone public.

He said he wasn't the one who'd taken it to the press. He also said that he'd called me out in that meeting because he saw me as a go-to guy; he knew I could take it; he looked to me as a leader.

I told him that the team had great leaders in Jeter, A-Rod, and the rest.

He said I was a different kind of leader. He said I had a toughness that inspired everyone else. He said he liked my raw desire and my raw honesty.

I said I still didn't like being raked over the coals in the New York newspapers.

He said New York was New York. The press was brutal, the fans were brutal, but he knew I was stronger than all that.

"When you told me you'd dominate this league," he said, "I called you arrogant. But now that you're making good on your promise, I see you as the strongest guy on this team. We're counting on you, Shef."

Just like that, our bad meeting turned good.

That year, in spite of a severe injury to my left shoulder, I hit thirty-six home runs and 121 RBIs. I led the team in slugging percentage—.534—and runs scored, 117. In July, I played in the All-Star game for the eighth time. As the papers pointed out, this would also mark the first time in history that anyone has ever played in All-Star games with five different teams. I was proud of that record.

In September, I had a rough series in the division play-offs against the Twins. Fortunately, my teammates—and A-Rod in particular—picked up the slack.

We lost the opener 2–0, but came back to win game 2 in twelve innings. I managed a two-run homer. A-Rod, though, was the hero, going four for six with three RBIs.

Kevin Brown was tough in game 3 and we won it, 8–4.

Game 4 was tight. I lost an easy fly in the Metrodome, which gave the Twins a boost. We were down by four in the eighth when I singled, starting a rally that culminated with Ruben Sierra's three-run home run. We were tied at 5–5 in the eleventh. A-Rod blasted his second double in the final three innings.

I came to bat, hitting .222 in the series.

A-Rod stole third.

I was still batting when A-Rod stormed home on a wild pitch.

Mariano Rivera held the Twins in the bottom of the inning, and that was it.

A-Rod was the margin of difference. At that moment I was convinced he was the best player in baseball.

Bring on the Red Sox.

THE CORPORATION
COLLAPSES

You can analyze. You can theorize. You can come up with a million explanations. When it comes to slumps, everyone thinks they know why they happen.

I don't.

All I know is that they do happen.

Sometimes we fly, sometimes we fall, sometimes we streak, and sometimes we stall.

Happens in business, happens in the arts, happens in sports.

You want to understand why. You struggle to come up with a really intelligent reason why it's happening. You want to figure out how to stop it from happening.

Well, I'm not saying the theories might not be right. These analyses might be brilliant and right on the money. But when push comes to shove, you're still left with the mystery.

If you were hot yesterday, why are you cold today?

In the first three games of the 2004 American League Championship Series, the Yankees were hot. I was hot. In the first game I walloped two doubles off Curt Schilling and went three for four. Next two games I connected for six more hits. We were coasting three games to zip and on the verge of putting the Red Sox away. The Boston curse, potent since 1918, was more potent than ever.

In the bottom of the ninth of game 4, we were ahead 4–3. Rivera, world's best reliever, had been flawless. All we needed were three more outs.

But all Boston needed was a walk, a stolen base, and single to tie the game.

Then, in the bottom of the twelfth, Big Papi put one in the right-field seats, and that was it.

The crumbling of the Corporation began right there and then.

For the rest of the series, A-Rod went one for twelve; I went one for twelve; Jeter went three for fifteen.

Boston became the first team to come back from 3–0. They beat us in seven and swept the Cardinals in four. No more curse.

Was I disappointed?

Of course.

I joined the Yankees to win another World Series. I wanted an American League victory to go with my Marlins National League victory. The Yankees World Series victory was to be the crowning achievement of my career.

Do I have a good explanation of what went wrong?

Not really.

You can say we were too anxious, that the momentum changed, that their pitching improved while ours declined, that they were hitting while we weren't. You can say anything.

The fact is, we went cold. Ice cold.

Fans identify with their teams. If their team's a winner, they're a winner. If their team's a loser, they feel like losers. Fans have big expectations. If some guy's making $15 million, he's expected to perform. In some ways, he's expected to be perfect. There's little patience for a slump. Big salaries bring big resentment when the results on the field aren't big.

My heart went out to A-Rod, who's an amazingly talented player. The national press murdered him. The New York press found new ways to ridicule him. You can argue that the press is speaking for the fans, or you can argue that the press is provoking the fans. Either way, negative news sells.

In New York, where people do a lot of their reading on subways and buses, the papers battle each other to see who can be nastier. Snide headlines are a New York City specialty. Loss never brings compassion. It brings anger and finger-pointing.

Well, as Earth Wind and Fire pointed out, that's the way of the world. In the end, I accept it. The best I can do is pray a prayer of compassion for those who lack compassion. But that's not easy for me. I want to fight anger *with* anger, not with understanding. I want to lash out at those who lash out at me.

I don't want to turn it over to God.

I don't want to love my enemies.

I want to fight back, to dominate, to win at any cost.

But the Spirit has nothing to with winning.

The Spirit is only about love.

And when you lose a big series, love is the last thing you're thinking about. What you're thinking about is revenge.

REWARDS

The Spirit is a quiet thing. That's challenging because I'm outspoken and loud. I can also be shy and withdrawn. But when it's time to say my piece, I'm going to be heard.

The Spirit is a subtle thing. That's also challenging because I'm not subtle by nature. The way I think and talk is obvious. Sometimes my thinking and talking can drown out the Spirit.

But the Spirit stays constant. I can call on it. I can lean on it. I can depend on it to keep me from doing something crazy. I can count on it to keep me out of my own way.

Example:

It was my second season with the Yankees. After playing 2004 with essentially one arm, I had shoulder surgery in the winter. By spring training I was feeling fine.

Steinbrenner, though, still hadn't responded to my demand

that I earn interest on my deferrals—even after a high-performance season where I played in 154 of 162 games. All during 2004, my torn shoulder meant that I had to throw sidearm and couldn't catch a fly ball over my head. Somehow, though, I made it work. I never asked for time off; I never asked to be the DH. I sucked it up. And because of my numbers, many thought I'd win MVP. When I didn't win, many thought it was because I never buttered up the press.

Given my achievements, I figured George would call me in and say, "Great year, Gary, you did what you promised. Now I'll do what I promised," and that would be it.

Instead George had his money man call me in. I didn't particularly want to see him. I wanted to see George. It was Steinbrenner who, a year before, had said to me, "Any big problem, bring it to me and we'll work it out man to man."

Instead George was now saying, "Work it out with my underling."

Doc told me not to worry. George meant well.

"George is getting up in years," said Doc. "He might not remember everything he promised you."

"Well, I'm *helping* him remember," I shot back.

But George wouldn't see me, and I was forced to see his money man.

"No interest on deferrals," said the money man. "We're keeping the contract the way it is."

I didn't even reply.

I just walked out.

Leaving the stadium, I walked past an ESPN truck. A reporter was talking on camera about me. He was saying the Yankees were having the same troubles the Dodgers had had. The implication was clear: Sheffield's greedy.

How did ESPN know about my negotiations? I sure hadn't told them. But someone in the Corporation obviously had.

Why?

Because if the press made me look bad, maybe I'd agree to the Yankees' terms and forget George's promise.

I'd had enough. I called my man Rufus Williams and said, "Tell them, 'Either pay the interest or look for another right fielder.' "

They paid the interest. And I left it there.

The Spirit said, "Move on. Leave it alone. Play the game."

I was playing a game at Fenway Park when the Spirit helped out again. I was going after a ball that Jason Varitek had hit down the line. I was at the wall when a fan took a swipe at me and smacked the side of my face. I made sure the ball was in my glove before I turned, swung at the guy and threw the ball back to the infield. Varitek beat the throw to third.

After the play, security jumped in the stands. I was headed back in that direction, not to attack the man, but to let him know I was standing my ground. He wasn't intimidating anybody. By then, though, officers stood between us and I never got a good look at the assailant.

Without the Spirit, I would have beat him to a pulp.

With the Spirit, I left it alone.

Baseball didn't want to leave it alone. They had to investigate to make sure I hadn't assaulted anyone. They confirmed I hadn't. I'd told them that from the get-go—and the photos said the same thing—but baseball has to protect baseball's image.

I put the incident out of mind and put together a solid 2005. During the year, though, rumors started flying—no doubt started by the Corporation—that the Yanks were looking to trade me. I figured the team was using the press to float the idea.

I used the press to sink the idea. I had reporters gather round and in clear language said, "Any team who trades for me isn't going to be happy, cause I'm not going to be happy. I'm only going to be happy if I stay where I am."

That ended the trade talk.

. . .

The Yankees' locker room is an interesting place. It's where the players' individual personalities are expressed.

Take Jeter. Derek's amazing. He's always in a good mood. His temperament is even and he makes everyone comfortable. That's a great gift. Being biracial, he relates to all his teammates, no matter what their background. You gotta love the guy.

A-Rod and Randy Johnson are superstars. You can feel them carry that role. Superstardom is a blessing, but also a burden. There are ridiculously high expectations these guys have to meet. You can practically see the weight on their shoulders. As a result, they learn to keep their distance. It's hard for them to have fun, hard to loosen up.

Jorge Posada is a fiery guy. I love his energy and combative nature. He'll challenge a pitcher who throws at his head. He'll never shy away from a fight. Every team needs a Posada.

Jason Giambi is someone who lives life to the fullest. Big heart. But when he goes through tough times, Jason needs a helping hand.

Everyone needs a helping hand. Because I was a seasoned vet with a long record and experience on many teams, I was happy to extend that helping hand to my teammates. I was a guy you could come to for straight-up answers to questions about what was bothering you on and off the field.

During team meetings, you often felt the tension.

I remember once we were in a deep slump. Derek called a team meeting. Because Derek is a pleasant man and upbeat captain, he talks in positive terms. Maybe even clichés. Things will get better. The rain will stop and the sun will shine. Every cloud has a silver lining.

I don't talk that way. And on this particular day, I could feel that someone needed to say what was really happening.

"I'm talking for the hitters," I began, "and I'm saying that all of us are doing too much complaining. We have a million excuses but excuses don't win ballgames. Hits do. We gotta stop moaning and groaning. We gotta stop crying like babies. We gotta go out there and get deep into the counts. Make the pitchers work. Be patient. Be smart. Be focused. And cut out the bellyaching."

After I talked for the hitters, Mariano Rivera talked for the pitchers. He said the same kind of thing—no excuses, just action.

The Yankees don't always get that kind of direct talk. But when they do, they respond well.

As a team, the Yankees are a funny group.

On a day off, the guys would occasionally go out for dinner. We'd be eating steaks in a quiet corner of a nice restaurant. Each of us would have something to say about the Yankees organization. The players would be highly critical of the corporate vibe that defines Steinbrenner, Inc.

Yet these same guys—intelligent men with strong opinions and great integrity—would silence themselves the very next day when confronted by the press. They're interested in protecting their image.

Maybe I should have learned something from them, but I never did. I saw public relations image making and plain-spoken truth as opposing forces.

The Yankees' image of perpetual winners was sustained that year when we wound up winning our division by six and a half games over Boston. I wound up hitting .291, with thirty-four homers and 123 RBIs. I was among the top ten vote-getters for the MVP. And I was still looking for a New York World Series ring.

But I didn't find it.

The Angels whipped us 3–2 in the division series.

I had a decent series with six hits. Vladimir Guerrero had a

superb series, hitting .333. His fielding was tremendous. Bengie
Molina was even better at bat; his average was .444.

But the Angels got cold and the White Sox stayed hot and
wound up winning their first World Series in eighty-eight years.
You couldn't help but feel happy for Chicago fans.

I didn't get the reward of another ring, but my record spoke
for itself.

Three strong years with the Dodgers.

Two strong years with the Braves.

Two strong years with the Yankees.

The way I saw it, I didn't have to prove myself again.

But the Yankees saw it differently.

WHAT'S REAL?

always thought it was things you can see. That's why I decided to study real estate. Land, buildings, and houses are things you can see and touch. Based on history, trends, and intelligent analysis, you can evaluate a property's worth and predict a property's potential. For the past several years I've pursued real estate investing with keen curiosity.

When I figured I knew enough to start speculating, I jumped in. I was cautious but also aggressive. I did well. In fact, I did well enough to retire from baseball and still have a thriving business with interests all over the country. I love the challenges and complexities of building a prosperous real estate portfolio. I'm hands-on, and I intend to keep at it for the rest of my working life.

That's real.

My family is real. My relationships with all my children

deepen every day. In 2006, DeLeon gave birth to our second son, Noah. Being a father of six is an awesome and beautiful responsibility.

My marriage was real from the beginning, and it's real today. I've seen real love between a man and a woman change into a mature love that changes me, even as it changes D.

My ability to play ball is real. My ability to earn big money as a player is also real. That's why at the start of the 2006 season, when Yankees General Manager Brian Cashman called me into his office, I was happy to hear him say that he saw nothing that would prevent the team from picking up my $13 million option in 2007.

But true to Yankees fashion, he told me one story, then spun it differently to the press.

For my part, I didn't even know why the press had to be involved. Why couldn't this conversation be private, not public?

But the reporters knew all about our meeting. Once again the Yankees had tipped them off. And naturally the reporters were looking for a negative angle.

"Are you disappointed," they wanted to know, "that Cashman didn't pick up your option right here and now?"

"Cashman was great," I said, intending to stay positive. "He said there's no reason why they wouldn't pick it up."

But when the press ran to Cashman, he started backing off. "We made Gary no guarantees," he said. "We promised him nothing."

Suddenly I was standing there with egg on my face.

The press had me sounding positive, and the press had Cashman sounding negative. And of course the press would have liked nothing more than to drive a wedge between Cashman and me. The press was looking to fuel the fire.

Cashman called and apologized to D and me. I accepted. I said, "Forget it, man. Let's just go out there and win."

The season started well. After the first four weeks, I was hitting .309. Then, on April 29, I collided with Toronto first baseman Shea Hillenbrand and tore a ligament on my left wrist. That required surgery and a cast that went up to my elbow. The injury kept me out for over a hundred games.

Meanwhile, the Yanks acquired Bobby Abreu from the Phillies. I warmly welcomed him to the team, and, like everyone, I was thrilled when he had a big season playing my right field position. Like everyone, I wanted a World Series ring and Bobby was doing more than his part to make that happen.

When my wrist healed and I finally got back into action, Torre asked whether I'd mind playing first base. I was hesitant. I'd never played first before, and first was where I'd had that collision. First base means continual contact. Another injury could mean the end of my career. But I agreed.

Part of the reason I agreed was Don Mattingly, Yankees coach. I love Don. He's a guy you must respect. He was one of the best first basemen ever, and he took me under his wing to show me the ins and outs of the position. Don was encouraging and, in spite of some residual problems with my wrist, I took on the challenge.

Those season-ending games were fun. I was feeling more and more comfortable at first. I had a three-run homer that gave me my 1,500th RBI. I was thinking like a kid again. It felt new, felt fresh, felt like fun. Though I'd never played first, in years past I'd stand at first during practice just to receive throws from the infielders. The little boy in me was alive and well. And Don couldn't have been more supportive.

We went into the play-offs against the Tigers with high hopes.

We beat them the first game—our bats were blazing—8–4. Derek had five hits, Abreu four RBIs, Giambi homered, and I knocked in a run.

Then we collapsed.

I had a disappointing series—only one hit, coming in the first game. A-Rod also slumped, and, for the most part, during those three straight losses, we were terrible.

Torre benched me in the third game. In the fourth game, he relegated A-Rod to eighth in the order. The man many think is the best player in baseball was suddenly hitting in the spot before the DH.

In my opinion, that sent a signal to Detroit that we were reeling and unsteady. It bolstered their confidence. Detroit manager Jim Leyland, the man who'd motivated me and the Marlins to a World Series in 1997, was motivating the Tigers like crazy. Jim's the best motivator I know. Motivation isn't Torre's greatest skill.

No excuses. Our offense was nonexistent. At one point we went twenty innings without scoring. In terms of emotional energy, though, we were not only outhit, but outmanaged.

The Tigers would go on to lose the series to the Cards, but Leyland was named AL manager of the year. He deserved it. His success brought to mind all he'd done for us down in Florida.

Up in New York, it became clear that the Yankees had no more use for me, other than as a pawn in a trade.

But after a lifetime in professional ball, I wasn't about to be a pawn. That's not my style.

FROM PINSTRIPES
TO TIGER STRIPES

enjoy the give-and-take of negotiations.

When I became my own agent and decided to use Rufus Williams as a financial advisor, I did so not out of ego but out of confidence. I had street sense, and I didn't mind mixing it up with the big boys in the boardroom.

Deal-making is a game, and the game can be fun. The game is also calculating. The Yankees love to use the press in their calculations, and I see the press's value as well.

The Yankees made statements about controlling my fate with the fourth-year option I'd given them. They said that once they picked up that option they could send me wherever they wanted. They used the press to put out their message.

I put out a countermessage. I said I wouldn't be happy to simply have my single option year picked up. I wanted a three-year contract with a team. At age thirty-eight, I knew this would be my seventh and final team, the team where I'd hit my five hundredth home run.

I had no bitterness toward the Yankees, but neither did I have great love. Steinbrenner is cold-blooded. So is Cashman. As many others have pointed out, Torre is an owner's manager, not a player's manager. Time and again, he's gone with ownership, not friendship, in making decisions. Torre is a company man, and the company he works for is George Steinbrenner, Inc.

At the same time, my time with the Yankees had been positive. For each of my two healthy years with the team I drove in over 120 runs and hit more than thirty homers. I had no regrets.

But if the Yankees were picking up my option to trade me for their advantage, I was going to take advantage of the press just as aggressively as they were.

My public statements made one thing clear: I wanted to go where *I* wanted to go. I wanted a winning team that suited my style. Otherwise I wouldn't be happy. And everyone knows that an unhappy player never performs at his very best. Owners got the message.

The Yankees picked up my option and put out the word that they wanted to trade me.

Then they made their statements to the press.

Then I made mine.

The Yanks acted like I had no control over anything.

But I kept talking and gave out the word: I wasn't about to go just anywhere.

My word worked. I got what I wanted: a trade to the GM and manager who had engineered the Marlins World Series win in 1997: Dave Dombrowski and Jim Leyland, the brilliant brain trust of the Detroit Tigers. There's no two men I'd rather play for; these are guys I love.

The Yankees got three pitchers, and I found myself in an ideal position, going to a powerhouse Tigers team that, in my mind, has a great chance to win all the gold in 2007.

Besides, I got a raise. In addition to picking up my $13 million option for 2007, the Tigers will be paying me $14 million in '08 and another $14 in '09. To cap off my career with a $41 million deal and the highest annual salary of my professional life gives me great satisfaction.

I'm grateful for the new opportunity.

Never been more motivated.

Never been more eager to give a team my all.

FORTY-MILLION-DOLLAR SLAVES

That's the title of a book I recently read. It's by Bill Rhoden, sportswriter for the *New York Times*. I liked it because it pulled no punches. The title got to me. I took it to mean that no matter how rich you are, you're still not in control.

For much of my career, that's how I've felt. I know some will say that sounds spoiled. People will point out that the system has improved. There's free agency. There's a players' association. There are huge contracts.

"Why don't you just shut up, Gary, and enjoy all the money you're making?" a friend recently said to me. "You got nothing to complain about."

But that attitude implies money is everything. If you make money you should be satisfied. You should ignore the injustices you see, the double-dealing, the hypocrisy, the racism, the history of exploitation.

"At the beginning of the 2006 Major League Baseball season," Rhoden writes, "four of thirty big league managers were African Americans. There were no African American owners. The most alarming statistic is that the percentage of black baseball players in the majors had dropped to 9 percent. They are largely excluded from ownership, which creates a domino effect. As sports became a multibillion-dollar enterprise, African Americans were largely shut out—shut out of front-office positions, presidencies, vice presidencies, and a wide variety of positions that flow into sports."

When a black man, no matter how great his talent, is put on the block and sold to the highest bidder, he can't help but feel historical echoes. If you're sensitive, if you learn about the past, if you listen to your elders—as I listened to my grandfather—you know that some things haven't changed.

I wanted to stay in San Diego, but I was sold. I wanted to stay with the Marlins, but I was sold. I wanted to deal with the Dodgers without being manipulated and bad-mouthed to the press. I wanted to negotiate with the Yankees, as most businessmen negotiate, in private and with goodwill. None of this happened, because the culture of baseball prevented it from happening.

The culture of baseball is based on exploitation. And just because salaries have ballooned doesn't mean that another form of exploitation—maybe even a nastier form—doesn't still exist.

It hurts my heart that few black men become franchise players. What was stopping me, for example, from becoming the franchise player in Florida or Los Angeles? The plain fact is that white owners want white franchise players. White men want white sons.

Only a fool would argue that white men haven't had troubled relationships with black men. I've seen it in my own life, over and

over again. When my dad, Harold Jones, world's most conscientious worker, became a manager and administrator, he was given
the power to hire and fire. He worked for the same company for
nearly thirty years without missing a day. He was on the verge of
retiring and looking forward to his pension. He took off a few
days to visit me—I was in San Diego then—and watch me play.
Around that same time, I bought him a Porsche. Dad usually
drove his truck to work, but on this particular day the truck was
in the shop, so he took the Porsche. That's the day he got fired.
The bosses claimed he took off too many days. The implication
was clear: Your son is Gary Sheffield and you drive a Porsche.
Why should we shell out all this money for your pension? We'll
fire you just before you hit thirty years and you'll walk away with
nothing.

"Sue them, Dad," I urged.

But Dad isn't the suing kind. He wouldn't do it.

"Fine," I said, "but I'm never going to let you work for a
white man again."

And he never has.

In America, the way Dad was treated happens every day in a
thousand ways.

When Grandpa taught me and Dwight baseball, he taught us
the social history as well. We learned about the evils of the past.
When I went out in the world, I learned that those evils still exist.
At first, that drove me crazy. I ranted and railed against all the
inequities I faced. I don't apologize for those outbursts. They
came out of a sense of outrage and a respect for equality.

When I found the Calmness, when I found love in God and
in a woman I admire and respect, when I assumed responsibility
for my family and responsibility for my growth as a Christian, I
became a changed man. But that change, that sense of Jesus living inside me, didn't—and still doesn't—diminish my need to call
it like I see it.

Being calm and being candid don't cancel each other out.

People always want to know how I compare myself to players like DiMaggio. Wasn't it tougher back then? Don't their stats mean more than ours?

"DiMaggio played against other white men," I say. "If he had to play against blacks or, in this era, Latinos and Asians—guys like Jeter, A-Rod, and Suzuki—he'd find the competition more intense. DiMaggio was incontestably great, but today baseball is international."

I thought of that international idea when I went to the 2005 All-Star Game in Comerica Park in Detroit. I was feeling good. This was my ninth All-Star appearance. The players were holding flags representing their different home countries. I noticed that not a single African American was holding a flag. That said something to me. That said that baseball is shoving us out. Baseball is cutting out recruitment programs in our neighborhoods. Baseball is looking elsewhere for talent. Baseball no longer cares about the talent in its own backyard.

I've been a professional player for over twenty years. The longer I play, the worse this subtle and not-so-subtle racism has grown.

It gives me no pleasure to report that the game I love is turning its back on my people.

THE PLEASURE
OF THE MOMENT

The moment can be the smell of freshly mowed grass at the start of a new season.

The moment can be waiting for the long lazy fly ball to land in my mitt.

The moment can be the sweet spot of the bat meeting the ball and sending it sailing over the moon.

The moment can be a perfectly executed double play, a throw to home plate that nails the runner, a well-executed bunt, a devastating slider that fools the slugger.

The moment can be looking over in the stands and seeing a father explaining the game to his son and daughter.

The beautiful baseball moments are many.

The moments last forever, from season to season, from family to family, from generation to generation.

. . .

In this moment, I'm listening to one of DeLeon's CDs. She's singing a song called "Faith Is." The song quotes the Bible. The message is, "Faith is the substance of things hoped for, the evidence of things not seen."

We worship the invisible.

We believe in the unseen.

We follow the music—and the heart—when the rhythm leads us to the righteous path.

D sings, "You are the breath I breathe. Your love is all I need."

D sings, "My life needed direction, and you made it right."

As much as D loves me, D isn't talking about me.

I'm listening to her music.

I'm listening to the Spirit. The Calmness is all over me.

I'm driving in my car.

Tampa looks beautiful. The bay is calm, the day serene. My phone rings.

It's Dwight.

Dwight's been fighting the good fight. For a while, he had to go away.

"You okay, bro?" I ask.

"I'm okay. Just wanted to hear your voice."

"Glad you called, Doc," I say. "Been thinking about you."

"You have?" he asks.

"Been thinking of those long-ago days. Those summer days when you burned in those pitches until my hand almost fell off."

Doc laughs. "Sorry about that, Gary."

"Nothing to be sorry about. You made me. Without you, I'd be working the night shift at Seven-Eleven."

"Oh, come on . . ."

"Seriously, those days made me."

"I feel like I let you down," he says. "Feel like I let down lots of people."

"We're all forgiven people, Doc. That's how it works. The past is gone. Forgotten. Besides, you did more for me than I can ever do for you. You're my uncle. I love and respect you as much today as I did when we were kids. You're still the baddest man to ever come out of Tampa."

"I don't know what to say—"

"I'll say it for you. I love you. And I love what Grandpa taught us when we didn't even know what the words meant."

"You mean Inside Power?"

"You got it, Doc. We all got it."

INDEX

Stockton, California, 67, 68
Strawberry, Darryl, 47, 50, 99,
    121, 177
Swindell, Greg, 115

Taiwan, 32–33, 35, 39
Tampa, Florida, 3, 10, 12, 34,
    38
Tampa Bay Buccaneers, 54
Taylor, Michigan, 40
Thome, Jim, 132
Toronto Bluejays, 82
Torre, Joe, 207–210, 222, 223,
    225
Trebelhorn, Tom, 85
Triple Crown, 101
Turner Field, 190

University of South Florida, 50,
    51

Varitek, Jason, 216
Vizquel, Omar, 131, 133

Walker, Kirk, 33
Walker, Larry, 208
Warner Brothers, 165
Werner, Tom, 103–104
White, Devon, 130, 133, 135,
    149
White, Paula, 191

White, Randy, 191
Wide World of Sports (ABC),
    32
Williams, Bernie, 207
Williams, Matt, 132
Williams, Rufus, 195–196,
    201, 202, 204, 205,
    216, 224
Williamsport, Pennsylvania,
    32, 37, 39, 40
Wilson, Mookie, 50, 65
Winans, Cece, 163
Winfrey, Oprah, 144, 163, 195
Without Walls International
    Church, Tampa,
    191–192
World Series, 10, 27, 64–66,
    120, 159, 174, 183,
    191, 192, 218–219
    Braves versus Marlins
    (1997), 131–135,
    137–138, 223
Wren, Frank, 175, 180–181
Wright, Big Jamey, 174
Wright, Jared, 133
Wrigley Field, 165–166

Yankee Stadium, 196, 206–207
Yount, Robin, 91–93

Zeile, Todd, 149